The Frogs Who Begged for a Tsar

(and 61 other Russian fables)

Лягушки, просящие Царя

(и ещё 61 русская басня)

Ivan Krylov
Иван Андреевич Крылов

Translated by Lydia Razran Stone
Лидия Разран Стоун, Переводчик

Illustrated by Katya Korobkina
Катя Коробкина, Иллюстрятор

Russian Life
BOOKS

ISBN 978-1-880100-55-4

Library of Congress Control Number: 2010939891

Russian Information Services, Inc.
PO Box 567
Montpelier, VT 05601-0567
www.russianlife.com
orders@russianlife.com
phone 802-223-4955
fax 802-223-6105

The night is full of cries and twitters –
The ass's bray, the owl's moan.
This cacophony of unseen critters
Should cheer us, for we're not alone.

While laughing at old Krylov's creatures
We notice traits that humans share
And see ourselves in many features
Of monkey, lion, fox and bear.

The author of these Russian fables
Lived far from us in place and time,
Yet had a vision that enables
Us to learn from each droll rhyme.

The beasts who prowl through his collection –
The eagles, squirrels, wolves and sheep –
Can tell us much in this connection,
For human nature's but skin deep.

Although we deem ourselves superior
To Krylov's ants and dragonflies,
We've but to peer at our interior
To find their foibles – human size.

Despite the common misconception
That humans are the master race,
We can't sustain our self-deception
When fauna feign a human face.

So set aside your patronizing
Ideas of roosters, nightingales,
And soon you'll find yourself realizing
What truth there is in Krylov's tales.

Lydia Razran Stone

Contents

* Fables by Krylov that are based on Aesop and/or La Fontaine.

Translator's Introduction

The fables of Ivan Krylov, of which the 62 presented here represent approximately 30 percent of his lifetime output, have been among Russia's most popular poems ever since they were written in the early nineteenth century. They are considered great entertainment for both children and adults, and their message has been found relevant during Tsarist, Soviet, and post-Soviet times. One or another edition of Krylov's addictive, edifying tidbits has been continuously available to the Russian reading public since 1809. Although Krylov has nothing like the literary stature that Shakespeare enjoys in English-speaking countries, as a source of phrases and aphorisms that have entered the Russian language, his influence upon his native tongue is roughly analogous to that of the great bard.

Ivan Andreyevich Krylov was born in 1769 into a family that was situated at the very bottom of the noble class (for bravery his father had been promoted from common soldier to officer). His father died when he was ten, leaving him virtually no inheritance, but for a trunk full of books. All but lacking any formal education, in his teens Krylov had the good fortune to impress a professional writer with his literary talent. This patron had him tutored alongside his own children and allowed the teenager free access to the conversation of writers and artists of the day.

As was normal for young men of the noble class, Krylov was assigned to a series of civil service jobs, some of which he actually performed more than nominally. His less than stellar impressions of the efficiency and integrity of civil servants are reflected in many of his fables. He also served as secretary and children's tutor to a rich nobleman. During his early adult years he wrote a number of satirical and tragic dramas and other literary works, some of which enjoyed moderate success. He also started a monthly satirical journal, which lasted less than a year and incurred the displeasure of Catherine the Great.

In 1805, Krylov published some translations of La Fontaine's fables into Russian verse; subsequently he gradually turned to adapting existing fables as well as writing original ones on more Russian themes. (The fables in this collection that are based on Aesop and/or La Fontaine are marked with an asterix.) By 1808, Krylov had virtually abandoned other literary forms in favor of creating fables. These works were an immediate success and brought him the fame that has lasted until this day. By 1835 he was named by Vissarion Belinsky as one of the four classics of Russian literature (along with Pushkin, Derzhavin and Griboyedov).

In 1812, Krylov was appointed to a post at the St. Petersburg Library, the largest and most prestigious in the country and one of the major centers of cultural life, where he served for 29 years. This post, along with his literary success, allowed him to live in comfort, calm and security until his death in 1844. During his lifetime, Krylov was famous for his wit, good humor, enormous appetite, and his sloppiness. He was frequently called the "laziest man in Russia." He never married.

Krylov's fables represent a combination of satire, rational moralizing, and details of Russian rural and provincial life, with an admixture of lyricism. The satire and moralizing are directed against the kind of universal human foibles portrayed by Aesop and La Fontaine, e.g., greed or susceptibility to flattery, but also against corruption, misuse of power and what might be called a poor work ethic. The fables, understandably, appear to have been heavily influenced by the ideals of the Enlightenment – espousal of progress and science, celebration of freedom and condemnation of injustice. In them, morality is justified more on the basis of rational self-interest and social good than on any underlying religious principles or emotional appeals to empathy. Many of the fables' implicit or explicit morals can be summarized by "as you sow, so shall you reap." Good (which in Krylov is most frequently wise) actions or decisions have good consequences, while bad or unwise ones lead to trouble. Getting the job done right and in a way that serves the common good is one of the most frequently extolled positive values. "True art," as embodied in the nightingale, is another. Absolute power is virtually always associated with injustice, corruption and/or cruelty. Hypocrisy of all kinds is frequently satirized.

Many of Krylov's fables are known to refer to historical events and figures. Krylov, of course, lived through the French invasion of Russia and its aftermath, and some of his more negative portrayals can be taken to refer to Napoleon or the French.

A number of Krylov's themes were eulogized in Soviet times by literary scholars and others. Most prominent among these is the emphasis on the important contributions made to the common good by "lowly" and anonymous work, and the respect due those who perform such work (i.e., the moles, ants, bees, tree roots, horses, and mice of the world). On the other hand, like many men of the Enlightenment, Krylov by no means espoused a democratically fluid (classless) society. While one of his most delightful fables, "The Geese," satirizes the idea that no one deserves deference because of his ancestors' accomplishments, many more satirize those who have ambitions to be something greater than they are by nature. In this collection "The Crow" is the clearest, but not the only, example of this theme. All the humble creatures Krylov extols, while aware of their own worth, also know and accept their places in the hierarchy. Of course the genre of fables fosters a view of rigidly demarcated strata of society. The moral to be derived from a crow attempting to be a peacock may or may not apply to a person of humble birth attempting to attain a higher place in society.

It has been said that Krylov is the first Russian writer whose works could be read by all (literate) strata of society, as well as by both adults and children. It is frequently pointed out that he uses three linguistic registers in his fables: neutral literary language in the majority of his descriptions, "folksy" colloquial language in the way many of his characters address each other, and a more exalted register in certain passages, such as the leaves' descriptions of their own virtues in the "Leaves and the Roots." Occasionally Krylov resorts to neoclassical trappings or references, as in those to Zeus in the fable that gives this volume its name. Krylov wrote in the language of his day, which, while containing some archaisms, presents minimal problems for anyone brought up reading nineteenth century literature in Russian, and, in accordance with his linguistic conservatism, is freer of French borrowing and influences than the works of many Russians of his time.

The verse in Krylov's fables is universally iambic (with, arguably, lapses in a very few lines). Other technical aspects of the poetry vary considerably between and within poems. In the current collection, poem length ranges between eight lines ("The Wolf and the Shepherds") and seventy ("The Frogs Who Begged for a Tsar"). Line length varies within the limits of six feet (12-13 syllables) and half a foot (one syllable). The poet imposes no requirement that rhyming lines be the same length, and this variation proves particularly effective in dialogue or when dialogue and description are interspersed. Within and between poems, rhyme schemes vary and this too serves to enliven the poetry.

In my translations I have adopted a somewhat unorthodox approach. Rather than attempting to make each translation conform to the specific original with respect to poem and line length and details of rhyme scheme, I have simply stayed within the limits Krylov (consciously or unconsciously) set himself in his entire body of work. I have, however, kept short fables short and long ones long. This approach has made my task as a translator substantially easier and allowed me to concentrate on other aspects of the translation. My conscious intention when I started translating was to use neutral literary language, except for dialogue, which would be more colloquial, though not dialectal. However, when I look back on my work I see that I, almost unconsciously, sprinkled the English with words and turns of speech more typical of nineteenth and early twentieth century poetry than of twenty-first century literary language, for example: *'twas, for naught, there to regale, a speck I scarce can see, ere flying to another just as base*. It is possible that use of such language will make the English translations less understandable to modern children and young people. On the other hand, the same might be said of the original Russian and children growing up speaking twenty-first century Russian. I also find that I have sometimes used modern idiomatic or colloquial phrases, especially in dialogue and morals, for comic effect. For example, the Sow in the "Sow Beneath the Oak" remarks about her favorite treat: "So let it die, what's that to me?... It's acorns that I care for – boy, do they taste good!" The moral of "The Cuckoo and the Rooster" similarly contains a thoroughly modern idiom (along with one that is nearly archaic today): "Just offer tit for tat – that's how you play this game."

I initially selected fables for inclusion in the book simply because I liked them and felt I could translate them. After I had completed a good number of translations, I set about making sure that the collection was representative of Krylov's work as a whole. So this collection contains: translations and adaptations from Aesop and/or La Fontaine, while the bulk are original to Krylov; satirical fables, both those that are primarily moralistic and those that are mostly for entertainment; fables based on universal values and ones that strikingly reflect those of the Enlightenment, as well as some that refer to historical events in Russia; late fables and early fables; long and short ones; fables with animals, Russian peasants, Greek gods, plants and even rocks and clouds as heroes.

A word about the illustrations: Our very talented illustrator, Katya Korobkina, who has spent her life in Russia, has seen innumerable "literal" illustrations of Krylov's fables and furthermore considers the fables themselves so clear and full of detail that they do not require any more literal renderings. She thus chose another approach. Krylov's fables, while of course universal, represent a particularly Russian reality. This reality is alive and well today, perhaps nowhere more so than in a Russian provincial city. Early in our work together, Katya set out on a sightseeing tour through one such city, a tour with pencil and sketch book, where she hoped to and actually did find modern day settings for Krylov's characters and situations. She ended one letter to me with the words, "Just look around you carefully and you will see all the heroes of these fables on the streets of your city." Just look carefully at Katya's illustrations; we think you will find they add a delightful and specifically Russian new dimension to Krylov's work.

Finally, I would like to express my gratitude to: my publisher, Paul Richardson, for his faith in me and his patience, as well as the astonishing efficiency with which he turned this book from a pipe dream into a reality; our illustrator, Katya Korobina, for her vision and willingness to accommodate her conceptions to mine; my husband Ned Stone for his support throughout this creative process and indeed our whole lives; my partner in rhyme, Vladimir Kovner, for his invaluable help and advice; my dear and learned friend, Anastasia Koralova, who edited and commented on every one of these translations; to Nora Favorov, the English copyeditor for this task, for suggesting numerous improvements in the text; to Tamara Eidelman and Elana Pick, for official and unofficial copyediting of the Russian, respectively.

I dedicate this translation to my grandchildren, Benjamin and Alexandra Orli, and Carlos and Jamie Perez. May they and other children have the chance to read the poems their grandparents enjoyed, whatever their native languages.

I hope you enjoy our book. Feel free to contact me with comments and suggestions.

Lydia Razran Stone
lydiastone@verizon.net

Петух и Жемчужное Зерно

Навозну кучу разрывая,
Петух нашёл Жемчужное Зерно
И говорит: “Куда оно?
Какая вещь пустая!
Не глупо ль, что его высоко так ценят?
А я бы право, был гораздо боле рад
Зерну Ячменному: оно не столь хоть видно,
Да сытно”.

Невежи судят точно так:
В чём толку не поймут, то всё у них пустяк.

The Rooster and the Pearl

While pecking in a compost mound,
A Rooster came upon a Pearl
And cried, amazed, "What's this I found?!
It has no use in all the world!
What fools men are to treasure such
Tough grains that no one can digest.
Now, barley does not shine as much,
But fills the belly. Which is best?"

Thus, often in the world of man,
A fool deems useless what he cannot understand.

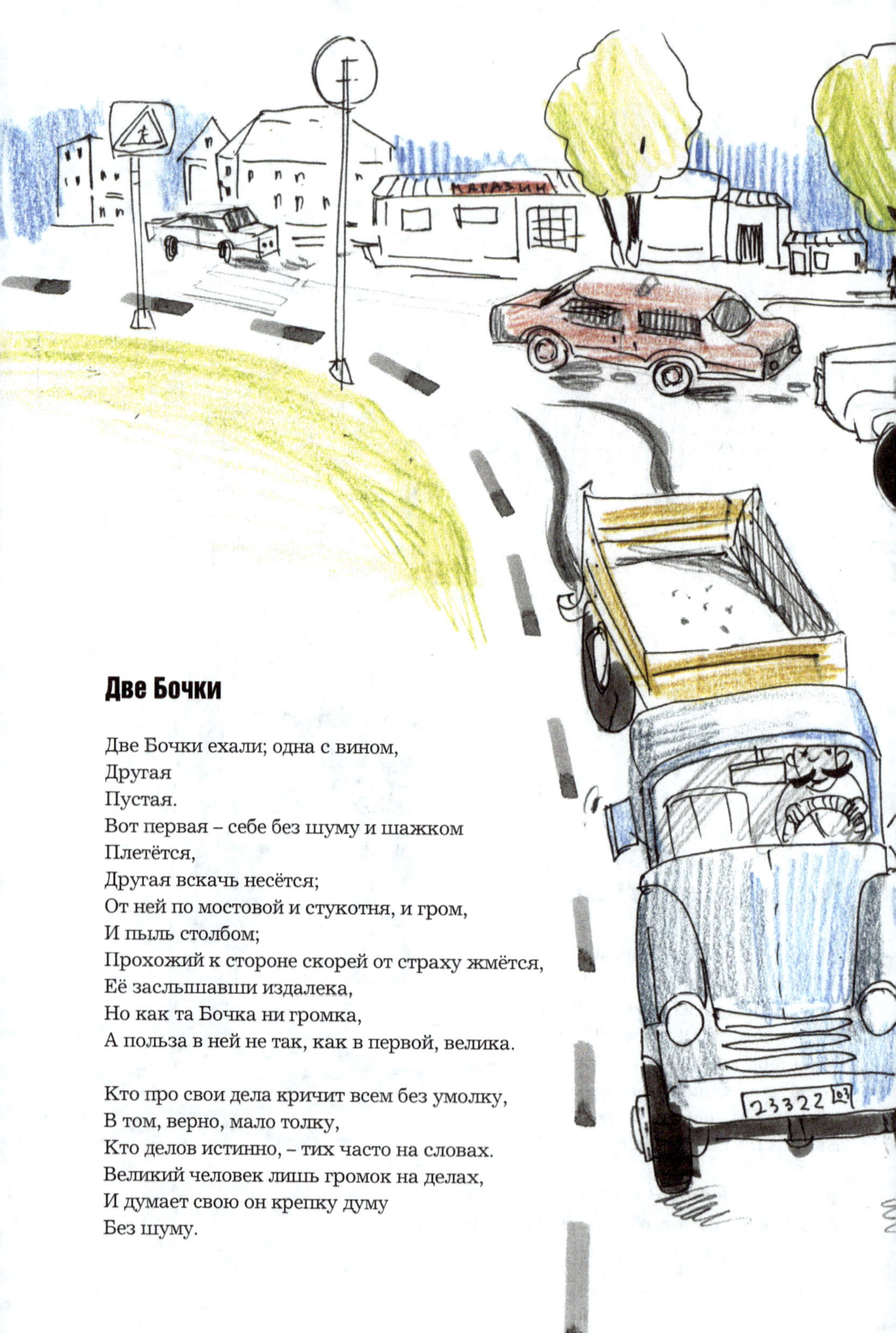

Две Бочки

Две Бочки ехали; одна с вином,
Другая
Пустая.
Вот первая – себе без шуму и шажком
Плетётся,
Другая вскачь несётся;
От ней по мостовой и стукотня, и гром,
И пыль столбом;
Прохожий к стороне скорей от страху жмётся,
Её заслышавши издалека,
Но как та Бочка ни громка,
А польза в ней не так, как в первой, велика.

Кто про свои дела кричит всем без умолку,
В том, верно, мало толку,
Кто делов истинно, – тих часто на словах.
Великий человек лишь громок на делах,
И думает свою он крепку думу
Без шуму.

The Two Barrel Carts

Two Barrel Carts were driving down a hill.
The first with wine was filled;
The second one held nothing but thin air.
The progress of the first was smooth and fair
And made a soothing sound.
The second bumped and lurched across the ground,
Which stirred the dust up in a cloud
And made a noise so loud
That people quaked with fear
And thought they heard a monster coming near.
But despite the empty barrel's din,
It was of far less worth than its full and quiet twin.

A person who declaims about his every deed
Is liable to be one we need not heed,
While one deserving of our praise
Prefers the worthy act to idle phrase.
And those who truly merit fame
Do not declaim.

Камень и Червяк

“Как расшумелся здесь! Какой невежа! –
Про дождик говорит на ниве Камень, лежа:
А рады все ему, пожалуй, – посмотри!
И ждали так, как гостя дорогого,
А что же сделал он такого?
Всего-то шёл часа два-три.
Пускай же обо мне расспросят!
Так я уж веки здесь: тих, скромен завсегда,
Лежу смирнёхонько, куда меня ни бросят,
А не слыхал себе спасибо никогда.
Недаром, право, свет поносят:
В нём справедливости не вижу я никак”. –
“Молчи! – сказал ему Червяк. –
Сей дождик, как его ни кратко было время,
Лишённую засухой сил
Обильно ниву напоил,
И земледельца он надежду оживил;
А ты на ниве сей пустое только бремя”.

Так хвалится иной, что служит сорок лет,
А проку в нём, как в этом Камне нет.

The Rock and the Worm

"What fools to fuss so over rain!"
A Rock who lay out in a field complained.
"Why should a shower cause such great ado?
Why welcome rain like some dear honored guest?
What has he done that all are so impressed?
He lingered but a trifling hour or two,
While on the other hand, take me;
I've lain here all my life, as steadfast as can be
And don't move from the spot where once men let me fall.
And do they thank me? Not at all.
No wonder people say that life's unfair.
It seems there is no justice anywhere."
"Be quiet!" cried a Worm who was nearby.
"The shower wasn't long, I won't deny,
But gave our poor parched field a thorough soak
And gave our farmers back their hope.
That rainfall, though quite short, our farm has healed,
While you're a useless burden on the field."

Some men who boast of serving long, and yet can name no yield,
Do nothing more of service than that rock out in the field.

Тень и Человек

Шалун какой-то тень свою хотел поймать:
Он к ней, она вперёд; он шагу прибавлять,
Она туда ж; он, наконец, бежать.
Но чем он прытче, тем и тень скорей бежала,
Всё не даваясь, будто клад.
Вот мой чудак пустился вдруг назад;
Оглянется, а тень за ним уж гнаться стала.

Красавицы! слыхал я много раз:
Вы думаете что? Нет, право, не про вас
А что бывает то ж с фортуною у нас;
Иной лишь труд и время губит,
Стараяся настичь её из силы всей;
Другой, как кажется, бежит совсем от ней:
Так нет, за тем она сама гоняться любит.

The Man and His Shadow

A man once tried to catch his shadow – just in play,
Or else to show who was the master.
He moved ahead, she moved away;
He tried to run, she just ran faster.
Discouraged, he turned round, and, looking back,
He found her in pursuit right on his track.

Fair ladies! I imagine it may seem
That you're the present fable's theme.
But you have got it wrong this time:
Good fortune's subject of this rhyme.
Some folks pursue her every day,
But fortune always slips away;
While others give her little thought
And find by fortune they are sought.

Белка

В деревне, в праздник, под окном
Помещичьих хором,
Народ толпился.
На Белку в колесе зевал он и дивился.
Вблизи с берёзы ей дивился тоже Дрозд:
Так бегала она, что лапки лишь мелькали
И раздувался пышный хвост.
“Землячка старая, – спросил тут Дрозд – нельзя ли
Сказать, что делаешь ты здесь?” –
“Ох, милый друг! тружусь день весь:
Я по делам гонцом у барина большого;
Ну, некогда ни пить, ни есть,
Ни даже духу перевесть”. –
И Белка в колесе бежать пустилась снова.
“Да, – улетая, Дрозд сказал – то ясно мне,
Что ты бежишь, а всё на том же ты окне”.

Посмотришь на дельца иного:
Хлопочет, мечется, ему дивятся все:
Он, кажется, из кожи рвётся,
Да только всё вперёд не подаётся,
Как Белка в колесе.

The Squirrel

A man who kept a Squirrel for a pet
Made sure its cage was set
So folks from miles around could come and see
And wonder at the beast who ran so busily.
He showed such zeal
Within his wheel
That his small paws were just a blur
And motion ruffled up his fur.
A Thrush upon a birch,
Observing from his perch,
Grew tired of admiring
And tried inquiring,
"My friend, your energy is stunning;
But why exhaust yourself with so much running?"
"I'm running errands for my boss,
A most important man of course.
I have no time to eat or rest,
Or even breathe, I am so pressed."
And saying this he started off to run again.
The Thrush flew off, remarking, "Well, it's clear.
You run like mad, but never get an inch from here."

There are like cases in the world of men,
Where someone runs and runs. But is his striving real?
Or does it get him nowhere like the Squirrel in the wheel?

Лебедь, Щука и Рак

Когда в товарищах согласья нет,
На лад их дело не пойдёт,
И выйдет из него не дело, только мука.

Однажды Лебедь, Рак да Щука
Везти с поклажей воз взялись,
И вместе трое все в него впряглись;
Из кожи лезут вон, а возу всё нет ходу!
Поклажа бы для них казалась и легка:
Да Лебедь рвётся в облака,
Рак пятится назад, а Щука тянет в воду.
Кто виноват из них, кто прав – судить не нам;
Да только воз и ныне там.

The Swan, the Pike and the Crab

When members of a team cannot agree;
Though each one labors conscientiously,
They'll not complete the task they've started on.

One day three beasts, a Pike, a Crab, a Swan,
Took on the job of hauling a full cart.
They got in harness set to make a start.
And each one pulled and pulled with all his might,
Each thinking that the way he pulled was right.
But lo! The cart just would not go,
Although the load was not that hard to tow.
The Pike sought water, Swan, of course, the sky,
While Crab a sideways course did ply.
Which one of them was right's not ours to judge.
As for the cart – it never budged.

Кукушка и Орёл

Орёл пожаловал Кукушку в Соловьи.
Кукушка, в новом чине,
Усевшись важно на осине,
Таланты в музыке свои
Выказывать пустилась;
Глядит – все прочь летят,
Одни смеются ей, а те её бранят.
Моя Кукушка огорчилась,
И с жалобой на птиц к Орлу спешит она.
"Помилуй! – говорит, – по твоему веленью
Я Соловьём в лесу здесь названа;
А моему смеяться смеют пенью!" –
"Мой друг! – Орёл в ответ, – я царь, но я не Бог.
Нельзя мне от беды твоей тебя избавить.
Кукушку Соловьём честить я мог заставить;
Но сделать Соловьём Кукушки я не мог".

The Cuckoo and the Eagle

King Eagle, to express his pleasure,
Named Cuckoo his "Official Nightingale."
The latter, proud beyond all measure,
Flew to a tree, there to unveil
The wondrous voice that, he felt sure,
Was granted with this sinecure.
But at his voice some laughed, some booed,
And all escaped fast as they could.
Poor Cuckoo, stung by this disdain,
Rushed off to Eagle to complain.
"Twas you who named me Nightingale, my king;
Is it not treason then to laugh at how I sing?"
"My friend," the Eagle with a smirk replied.
"I'm helpless to restore your pride.
Conferring titles on our friends is something all kings do:
But only God can truly make a Nightingale of you."

Бумажный Змей

Запущенный под облака,
Бумажный Змей, приметя свысока
В долине мотылька,
“Поверишь ли! – кричит, – чуть-чуть тебя мне видно;
Признайся, что тебе завидно
Смотреть на мой высокий столь полёт”. –
“Завидно? Право, нет!
Напрасно о себе ты много так мечтаешь!
Хоть высоко, но ты на привязи летаешь.
Такая жизнь, мой свет,
От счастия весьма далёко;
А я, хоть, правда, невысоко,
Зато лечу
Куда хочу;
Да я же так, как ты, в забаву для другого,
Пустого
Век целый не трещу”.

The Kite

Up in the sky a children's Kite
Could just make out from his great height
A moth down in a valley far below.
He yelled to her, "Hallo, Hallo!
From up here you're a speck I scarce can see!
Confess that you are envious of me,
Who soars at heights you never will attain."
"Me – envious? Are you insane?
You soar, it's true, but always on a lead.
Life on a leash, my friend,
Though high you may ascend,
Is an unhappy one, indeed.
But as for me,
I am quite free.
Though I fly low,
I choose where I will go.
And do not rise and fall
At someone else's beck and call."

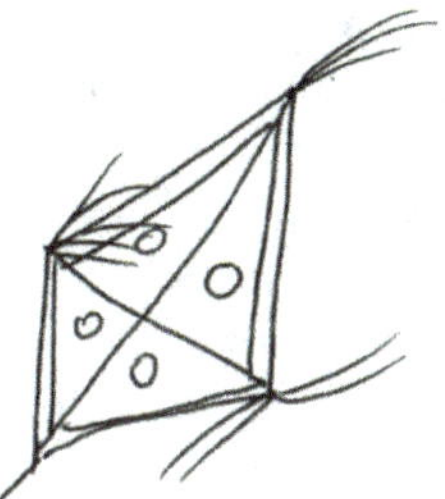

Орёл и Куры

Желая светлым днём вполне налюбоваться,
Орёл поднебесью летал
И там гулял,
Где молнии родятся.
Спустившись, наконец, из облачных вышин,
Царь – птица отдыхать садится на овин.
Хоть это для Орла насесток незавидный,
Но у Царей свои причуды есть:
Быть может, он хотел овину сделать честь,
Иль не было вблизи, ему по чину сесть,
Ни дуба, ни скалы гранитной;
Не знаю, что за мысль, но только что Орёл
Немного посидел
И тут же на другой овин перелетел.
Увидя то, хохлатая наседка
Толкует так с своей кумой:
"За что Орлы в чести такой?
Неужли за полёт, голубушка соседка?
Ну, право, если захочу,
С овина на овин и я перелечу.
Не будем же вперёд такие дуры,
Чтоб почитать Орлов знатнее нас.
Не больше нашего у них ни ног, ни глаз;
Да ты же видела сейчас,
Что понизу они летают так, как куры".
Орёл ответствует, наскуча вздором тем:
"Ты права, только не совсем.
Орлам случается и ниже кур спускаться;
Но курам никогда до облак не подняться!"

Когда таланты судишь ты, –
Считать их слабости трудов не трать напрасно;
Но, чувствуя, что в них и сильно, и прекрасно,
Умей различны их постигнуть высоты.

The Eagle and the Chickens

The King of Birds, the Eagle, flew
Above the earth, to dizzy heights one morn.
He swooped and soared, admiring the view
Aloft, where lightning storms are born.
Fatigued at last, back down the Eagle sped
And came to rest atop a common shed,
A perch, of course, unworthy of a king.
Perhaps he wished to show lack of conceit,
Or else could find no better, nobler seat –
An oak, a cliff or some such thing.
I cannot read his mind, but know that shed's the place
He sat, ere flying to another, just as base.
A Chicken, who on that small farm resided
Observed all this, then to her friend confided,
"Why does the world so honor every Eagle?
Their flight? Oh no, it's far from regal.
Why even I,
Were I to try,
Could fly
As well as that from shed to shed.
From now on let us not be fooled," she said,
"Into believing Eagles nobler than the rest.
Their legs and eyes are like in size to ours.
As for their fabled flying powers:
Now I have seen one fly, I'm not impressed."
Sick of these fools, the Eagle gave reply,
"That what you say is true I don't deny:
At times we Eagles may at Chicken level fly.
But more important: it is true
That Chickens never ever reach the heights we do."

So, when on greatness you reflect.
Don't waste your time on each defect,
As many petty people do,
But note instead what's fine and true.

Пчела и Мухи

Две Мухи собрались лететь в чужие краи.
И стали подзывать с собой туда Пчелу:
Им насказали попугаи
О дальних сторонах большую похвалу.
Притом же им самим казалося обидно,
Что их, на родине своей,
Везде гоняют из гостей;
И даже до чего (как людям то не стыдно,
И что они за чудаки!):
Чтоб поживиться им не дать сластями
За пышными столами,
Придумали от них стеклянны колпаки;
А в хижинах на них злодеи пауки.
"Путь добрый вам, – Пчела на это отвечала, –
А мне
И на моей приятно стороне.
От всех за соты я любовь себе сыскала –
От поселян и до вельмож.
Но вы летите,
Куда хотите!
Везде вам будет счастье то ж:
Не будете, друзья, нигде, не быв полезны,
Вы ни почтенны, ни любезны.
А рады пауки лишь будут вам
И там".

Кто с пользою отечеству трудится,
Тот с ним легко не разлучится;
А кто полезным быть способности лишён,
Чужая сторона тому всегда приятна:
Не бывши гражданин, там мене презрен он,
И никому его там праздность не досадна.

The Bee and the Flies

Two Flies, whose hearts were set on emigration,
Attempted to persuade a Bee to tag along,
For parrots told such tales of foreign nations,
That their desire to see these lands grew strong.
And with their homeland they were discontented,
Since they were never welcomed when they came to call.
By selfish people they were oft prevented
From sampling food (as if they'd eat it all).
And just to thwart them, screens had been invented,
And by fierce spiders they were much tormented.
"I wish you bon voyage," said Bee.
"My native land is good enough for me.
Here, honey's earned me honor and respect
From everyone – both low and high!
My honey pleases all – so that is why!
Good luck, to you. Though I suspect,
That things won't change, whatever land you choose,
For nowhere will you ever be of use.
So you will never be respected anywhere,
Though only spiders will be glad to see you there."

Those laboring to help their native land
Find emigration hard to understand.
But those who have no useful skills to share
Are apt to want to try their luck elsewhere.
They hope perhaps that no one there will guess
They choose to live their lives in idleness.

Гуси

Предлинной хворостиной
Мужик Гусей гнал в город продавать;
И, правду истинну сказать,
Не очень вежливо честил свой гурт гусиной:
На барыши спешил к базарному он дню
(А где до прибыли коснётся,
Не только там гусям, и людям достаётся).
Я мужика и не виню;
Но Гуси иначе об этом толковали
И, встретяся с прохожим на пути,
Вот как на мужика пеняли:
"Где можно нас, Гусей, несчастнее найти?
Мужик так нами помыкает,
И нас, как будто бы простых Гусей, гоняет;
А этого не смыслит неуч сей,
Что он обязан нам почтеньем;
Что мы свой знатный род ведём от тех Гусей,
Которым некогда был должен Рим спасеньем:
Там даже праздники им в честь учреждены!" –
"А вы хотите быть за что отличены?" –
Спросил прохожий их. – "Да наши предки..." – "Знаю,
И всё читал: но ведать я желаю,
Вы сколько пользы принесли?" –
"Да наши предки Рим спасли!" –
"Всё так, да вы что сделали такое?" –
"Мы? Ничего!" – "Так что ж и доброго в вас есть?
Оставьте предков вы в покое:
Им поделом была и честь;
А вы, друзья, лишь годны на жаркое".

Басню эту можно бы и боле пояснить –
Да чтоб гусей не раздразнить.

The Geese

A man was herding Geese
To market to be sold;
He drove them without cease.
Indeed, if truth be told,
He gave but little thought to being kind,
So pushed them hard with profit on his mind.
(Pursuit of which can often cause misuse
Of other creatures, Man as well as Goose.)
I hold the peasant blameless, for my part.
The flock of Geese, though, took this much to heart,
And, when a man passed by them on the lane,
Began at once to bitterly complain.
"More wretched Geese than we you'll never meet.
This peasant bullies us and shows us no respect.
Like common Geese he drives us through the dust and heat.
Oh, what a lout, he surely can't suspect
That deference and honor are our due;
For we descend directly from those heroes who
Saved Rome from ruin many years ago.
The Romans fete us yearly, they revere us so."
"And you, how have you honor earned?"
The passerby then asked.
"Our forebears..." "No, their story we've all learned.
But you, what's been your lives' main task?"
"Our forebears rescued Rome," a Goose began.
"Not them, but you, what good have you Geese done?"
Inquired the man.
"Why, none!"
"Well, then to honor you've no claim
And only have yourselves to blame.
Pray let your forbears rest in peace.
They have the right to boast.
But you, my friends, are fit to roast
Like any common Geese."

The moral of this tale I would explain,
But geese when riled are such a pain.

Орёл и Крот

Не презирай совета ничьего,
Но прежде рассмотри его.

Со стороны прибыв далёкой
В дремучий лес, Орёл с Орлицею вдвоём
Задумали навек остаться в нём
И, выбравши ветвистый дуб высокой,
Гнездо себе в его вершине стали вить,
Надеясь и детей тут вывести на лето.
Услыша Крот про это,
Орлу взял смелость доложить,
Что этот дуб для их жилища не годится,
Что весь почти он в корне сгнил
И скоро, может быть, свалится,
Так чтоб Орёл гнезда на нём не вил.
Но кстати ли Орлу принять совет из норки,
И от Крота! А где же похвала,
Что у Орла
Глаза так зорки?
И что за стать Кротам мешаться сметь в дела
Царь-птицы!
Так многого с Кротом не говоря,
К работе поскорей, советчика презря, –
И новоселье у царя
Поспело скоро для царицы.
Всё счастливо: уж есть и дети у Орлицы.
Но что ж? – Однажды, как зарей,
Орёл из-под небес к семье своей
С богатым завтраком с охоты торопился,
Он видит: дуб его свалился
И подавило им Орлицу и детей.
От горести не взвидя свету:
“Несчастный! – он сказал, –
За гордость рок меня так люто наказал,
Что не послушался я умного совету.
Но можно ль было ожидать,
Чтобы ничтожный Крот совет мог добрый дать?” –
“Когда бы ты не презрел мною, –
Из норки Крот сказал, – то вспомнил бы, что рою
Свои я норы под землей,
И что, случаясь близ корней,
Здорово ль дерево, я знать могу верней”.

The Eagle and the Mole

Examine well-meant counsel case by case –
Do not disdain it, even though its source is base.

King Eagle and his mate, in need of rest,
Once came upon a dense romantic wood,
Where they decided they would make a home for good
In towering oaks, just perfect for their nest.
So, picking out the one that they preferred,
They gathered grass and sticks, like any other bird,
In hopes of raising eaglets there by spring.
Now little Mole, who lived below,
Was told of this by his friend, Crow;
And, though he was a timid thing,
Resolved that he would tell the King
That, to protect his family,
He'd better choose another tree.
For this one's roots were full of rot
And it would fall soon, like as not.
But proud King Eagle paid no mind
To counsel from a lowly Mole,
Who lived his life in some dank hole,
And was, they said, quite blind.
And anyway how did he dare
To meddle in the King's affair?
So he ignored the Mole's advice
And got to work. And in a trice
The nest was all completed;
The Queen on eggs was seated;
And eaglets soon were born.
So all was grand, till one fine morn,
King Eagle, in a gracious mood,
Was bringing home some breakfast food,
When with dismay and grief he found
His oak had fallen to the ground
And crushed his family.
In bitter grief, King Eagle cried,
"I'm being punished for my pride
And for my snobbery.
But how could I have ever guessed
A lowly Mole would know what's best."
Mole said, "Disdain had made you blind.
If not you would have borne in mind
One simple thing:
That underground is where I dwell;
And so I know tree roots quite well
And if they're rotten I can tell
Much better than a king."

Булыжник и Алмаз

Потерянный Алмаз валялся на пути;
Случилось, наконец, купцу его найти.
Он от купца
Царю представлен,
Им куплен, в золоте оправлен
И украшением стал царского венца.
Узнав про то, Булыжник развозился,
Блестящею судьбой Алмаза он прельстился
И, видя мужика, его он просит так:
“Пожалуйста, земляк,
Возьми меня в столицу ты с собою!
За что здесь под дождём и в слякоти я ною?
А наш Алмаз в чести, как говорят.
Не понимаю я, за что он в знать попался?
Со мною сколько лет здесь рядом он валялся;
Такой же камень он, и мне набитый брат.
Возьми ж меня. Как знать? Коль там я покажуся,
То также, может быть, на дело пригожуся”.
Взял камень мужичок на свой тяжёлый воз,
И в город он его привёз.
Ввалился камень мой и думает, что разом
Засядет рядом он с Алмазом;
Но вышел для него случай совсем иной:
Он точно в дело взят, но взят для мостовой.

The Cobblestone and the Diamond

A Diamond someone lost lay on the public way
Until a merchant found it there one day
And took it to the tsar, who paid him lavishly
And set it in his crown for all to see.
On hearing of this, Cobblestone became convinced
That, in the city, he would also be a prince
And have the selfsame life the Diamond had.
He hailed a passerby, "Hey, lad,
Please take me to the capital with you.
Why should I suffer as I do,
Stuck here in mud and rain and snow?
Our Diamond's now a big shot there, you know.
Though how he won his rank, I don't quite see,
I bet the same could happen there to me.
For he was just a stone like all us others.
We long lay side by side; we were like brothers.
Who knows, when I get to the city,
They just might find that kind of post for me.
Then, like the Diamond, I'd be sitting pretty."
The fellow tossed him in his dray
And soon his trip was underway.
Once in the city, he surmised
That like the Diamond he'd be prized.
Indeed he got a post that very day:
To plug a pothole in the main highway.

Синица

Синица на море пустилась:
Она хвалилась,
Что хочет море сжечь.
Расславилась тотчас о том по свету речь.
Страх обнял жителей Нептуновой столицы;
Летят стадами птицы;
А звери из лесов сбегаются смотреть,
Как будет Океан, и жарко ли гореть.
И даже, говорят, на слух молвы крылатой
Охотники таскаться по пирам
Из первых с ложками явились к берегам,
Чтоб похлебать ухи такой богатой,
Какой-де откупщик и самый тароватый,
Не давывал секретарям.
Толпятся: чуду всяк заранее дивится,
Молчит и, на море глаза уставя, ждёт;
Лишь изредка иной шепнёт:
“Вот закипит, вот тотчас загорится!”
Не тут-то: море не горит.
Кипит ли хоть? – и не кипит.
И чем же кончились затеи величавы?
Синица со стыдом всвояси уплыла;
Наделала Синица славы,
А моря не зажгла.

Примолвить к речи здесь годится,
Но ничьего не трогая лица:
Что делом, не сведя конца,
Не надобно хвалиться.

The Titmouse

A Titmouse bragged she'd set the sea on fire.
(Who knows what it had done to earn her ire?)
The rumor of this threat spread far and wide,
And Neptune's subjects all were terrified.
The birds and beasts of land all came
To watch the ocean be consumed by flame.
The rumor brought gourmets and gluttons too,
All set to taste the sea transformed to free fish stew,
Which even palace chefs could never brew.
In silent wonder, crowds of creatures stood and gazed.
Though nothing yet had happened, still they felt amazed.
From time to time somebody would declare,
"It's boiling now, at any minute it will flare!"
But never did the ocean flare, or even glow.
At least it boiled? I'm sorry, no.
This great event, how'd it conclude?
The Titmouse slunk off, much subdued.
Though she had gained some fame (unearned).
As for the sea – it never burned.

The moral here's a simple one:
You should not brag until your deed is done.

Музыканты

Сосед соседа звал откушать;
Но умысел другой тут был:
Хозяин музыку любил
И заманил к себе соседа певчих слушать.
Запели молодцы: кто в лес, кто по дрова,
И у кого что силы стало.
В ушах у гостя затрещало
И закружилась голова.
"Помилуй ты меня, – сказал он с удивленьем, –
Чем любоваться тут? Твой хор
Горланит вздор!" –
"То правда, – отвечал хозяин с умиленьем, –
Они немножечко дерут;
Зато уж в рот хмельного не берут,
И все с прекрасным поведеньем".

А я скажу: по мне уж лучше пей,
Да дело разумей.

The Musicians

A rich man asked a friend to come and dine,
Inviting him for more than food and wine,
For he had had his servants form a choir,
That he was hoping that his neighbor would admire.
The singers entered and began to sing,
The poor guest's ears began to ring,
His head began to swim, since no one sang on key
Or tune. 'Twas pure cacophony.
The guest cried out, amazed,
"What is there to admire?
This choir
Is dire."
The host replied, unfazed,
"Well, yes, I know their singing stinks,
And yet not one among them drinks.
And no one can impeach
The morals shown by each."

Myself, I'd rather men who might get tight,
But had the proper skills to do things right.

Листы и Корни

В прекрасный летний день,
Бросая по долине тень,
Листы на дереве с зефирами шептали,
Хвалились густотой, зелёностью своей
И вот как о себе зефирам толковали:
“Не правда ли, что мы краса долины всей?
Что нами дерево так пышно и кудряво,
Раскидисто и величаво?
Что б было в нём без нас? Ну, право
Хвалить себя мы можем без греха!
Не мы ль от зноя пастуха
И странника в тени прохладной укрываем?
Не мы ль красивостью своей
Плясать сюда пастушек привлекаем?
У нас же раннею и позднею зарей
Насвистывает соловей.
Да вы, зефиры, сами
Почти не расстаётесь с нами”. –
“Примолвить можно бы спасибо тут и нам”, –
Им голос отвечал из-под земли смиренно.
“Кто смеет говорить столь нагло и надменно!
Вы кто такие там,
Что дерзко так считаться с нами стали?” –
Листы, по дереву шумя, залепетали.
“Мы те, –
Им снизу отвечали, –
Которые, здесь роясь в темноте,
Питаем вас. Ужель не узнаёте?
Мы – Корни дерева, на коем вы цветёте.
Красуйтесь в добрый час!
Да только помните ту разницу меж нас:
Что с новою весной лист новый народится,
А если корень иссушится, –
Не станет дерева, ни вас”.

The Leaves and the Roots

Within a valley famous for its trees,
One perfect summer morn,
The Leaves were chatting with the breeze
And blowing their own horn.
They praised themselves for thickness and for hue
And said, "Don't you agree that it is true
That we're the crowning glory of this place?
For don't we crown the treetops with our lace?
Who can deny, though it's a sin to boast,
Without its Leaves a tree is just a post?
Don't we protect the shepherds with our shade?
Does not the beauty that we lend the vale
Entice the girls to come dance in this glade?
And what of nightingale?
Is he not always singing from a tree?
Don't you, sweet breeze, seek out our company?"
Just then a voice came from beneath the earth below,
"You have forgotten us; you owe us thanks, you know."
The Leaves exclaimed (they took offense),
"Who dares address us with such insolence?"
The voice replied,
"We are the ones who in the darkness toil
To bring you nourishment from deep within the soil.
We are the Roots of that same tree where you reside
And show the world your beauty, like a bride.
We don't begrudge you this,
But please remember we exist
And serve a function different from display.
Each spring a crop of Leaves is born anew.
But if the Roots dry up or rot away,
The tree is sure to die and so will you."

Две Собаки

Дворовый, верный пёс
Барбос,
Который барскую усердно службу нёс,
Увидел старую свою знакомку,
Жужу, кудрявую болонку,
На мягкой пуховой подушке, на окне,
К ней ластяся, как будто бы к родне,
Он, с умиленья чуть не плачет,
И под окном
Визжит, вертит хвостом
И скачет.
“Ну что, Жужутка, как живёшь,
С тех пор, как господа тебя в хоромы взяли?
Ведь, помнишь: на дворе мы часто голодали.
Какую службу ты несёшь?” –
“На счастье грех роптать, – Жужутка отвечает, –
Мой господин во мне души не чает;
Живу в довольстве и добре,
И ем и пью на серебре;
Резвлюся с барином; а ежели устану,
Валяюсь по коврам и мягкому дивану.
Ты как живёшь?” – “Я, – отвечал Барбос,
Хвост плетью опустя и свой повеся нос, –
Живу по-прежнему: терплю и холод,
И голод,
И, сберегаючи хозяйский дом,
Здесь под забором сплю и мокну под дождём;
А если невпопад залаю,
То и побои принимаю.
Да чем же ты, Жужу, в случай попал
Бессилен бывши так и мал,
Меж тем как я из кожи рвусь напрасно?
Чем служишь ты?”
– “Чем служишь! Вот прекрасно! –
С насмешкой отвечал Жужу, –
На задних лапках я хожу”.

Как счастье многие находят
Лишь тем, что хорошо на задних лапках ходят!

Two Dogs

Old faithful Rex, who served as watchdog and as guard,
Once from his post inside his master's yard
Caught sight of Fifi, his old friend.
She looked the same – petite and fluffy still –
Upon a pillow on the windowsill.
His joy at this was without end.
He greeted her like some close long-lost kin.
"Well, Fifi my old pal, how have you been,
What's happened since the masters took you in
From our old life of hunger, wet, and cold?
How do you serve them? What position do you hold?"
She answered, "I cannot complain.
My master loves me so, it's quite insane.
A life of comfort has been given me by fate
He feeds me all my meals upon a silver plate.
We play until I'm ready for my nap
Upon soft cushions or his lap.
And you, dear Rex, how's life been treating you?"
With tail between his legs and lowered head,
The watchdog said,
"I lead the life I've always led,
Here in the yard.
The whole estate I guard
And sleep outside beneath the fence,
Through hunger, cold and rain.
And if I give offense,
I'm beaten with a cane.
But Fifi, of us all,
How did you win such favor, you so weak and small,
While I must work so hard
For no reward?
How do you serve? What is your skill?"
"My skill?" she answered from the windowsill,
"I will not lie, this favor comes because
I've learned to walk on my hind paws."

Men, too, win favor, fame, applause
If they can walk on their hind paws.

Слон и Моська

По улицам Слона водили,
Как видно, напоказ –
Известно, что Слоны в диковинку у нас –
Так за Слоном толпы зевак ходили.
Отколе ни возьмись, навстречу Моська им.
Увидевши Слона, ну на него метаться,
И лаять, и визжать, и рваться,
Ну так и лезет в драку с ним.
“Соседка, перестань срамиться, –
Ей Шавка говорит, – тебе ль с Слоном возиться?
Смотри, уж ты хрипишь, а он себе идёт
Вперёд
И лаю твоего совсем не примечает. –
“Эх, эх! – ей Моська отвечает, –
Вот то-то мне и духу придаёт,
Что я, совсем без драки,
Могу попасть в большие забияки.
Пускай же говорят собаки:
“Ай, Моська! знать, она сильна,
Что лает на Слона!”

The Elephant and the Pug

An Elephant was led along the avenue,
For no real cause, just entertainment's sake.
A crowd of people followed in his wake,
Since Elephants round here are rarely put on view.
Just then a Pug appeared upon his path
And, seeing him, began to bark in wrath
And rush at him as if to pick a fight.
A dog nearby said, when he saw this sight,
"Be still, who do you think you're harassing
He doesn't notice – it's embarrassing!
Just look, you've barked yourself all hoarse,
While he continues calmly on his course."
The Pug replied, "But don't you see, I've done enough
To earn a name as one who's brave and tough;
Without the need, I'll have you know,
To give or get a single blow.
Now all the other dogs will say
Each time they see me come their way:
'Here's Pug, who's brave and confident
And challenged a huge Elephant.'"

Мышь и Крыса

“Соседка, слышала ль ты добрую молву? –
Вбежавши, Крысе Мышь сказала, –
Ведь кошка, говорят, попалась в когти льву?
Вот отдохнуть и нам пора настала!” –
“Не радуйся, мой свет, –
Ей Крыса говорит в ответ. –
И не надейся попустому!
Коль до когтей у них дойдёт,
То, верно, льву не быть живому:
Сильнее кошки зверя нет!”

Я сколько раз видал, приметьте это сами:
Когда боится трус кого,
То думает, что на того
Весь свет глядит его глазами.

The Mouse and the Rat

"There is great news; rejoice, my friend,"
Proclaimed a Mouse to her good neighbor, Rat.
"You'll never guess what's happened to the Cat.
The Lion's caught her; now our woes are at an end."
Said Rat, "I fear rejoicing's premature.
If things come down to combat claw to claw,
The Lion won't survive, of that I'm sure:
No creature in the world could overcome Cat's paw."

I've seen it happen time and time again
That cowardice beclouds the minds of men.
And, in their blindness, cowards think it's clear
That all the world is scared of what they fear.

Кукушка и Петух

“Как, милый Петушок, поёшь, ты громко, важно!” –
“А ты, Кукушечка, мой свет,
Как тянешь плавно и протяжно:
Во всем лесу у нас такой певицы нет!” –
“Тебя, мой куманёк, век слушать я готова”. –
“А ты, красавица, божусь,
Лишь только замолчишь, то жду я, не дождусь,
Чтоб начала ты снова...
Отколь такой берётся голосок?
И чист, и нежен, и высок!..
Да вы уж родом так: собою невелички,
А песни-что твой соловей!” –
“Спасибо, кум; зато, по совести моей,
Поёшь ты лучше райской птички.
На всех ссылаюсь в этом я”.
Тут Воробей, случась, примолвил им: “Друзья!
Хоть вы охрипните, хваля друг дружку, –
Всё ваша музыка плоха!..”

За что же, не боясь греха,
Кукушка хвалит Петуха?
За то, что хвалит он Кукушку.

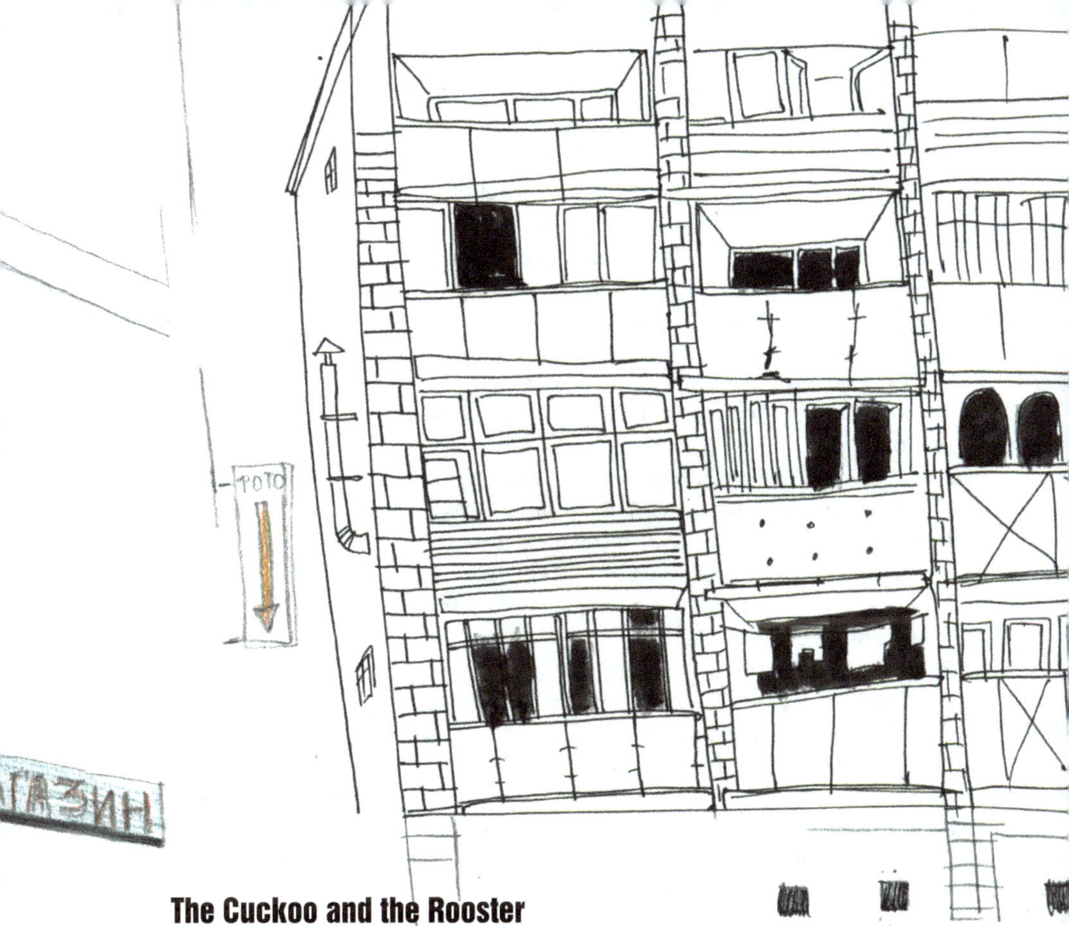

The Cuckoo and the Rooster

"How loud you sing, dear Rooster, and with what noblesse!"
"And you, my sweetest Cuckoo, I confess,
The notes that you produce are so prolonged,
In all the woods no one can match your song."
"To yours, friend Rooster, I could listen till I die."
"When you stop singing, fair one, I feel I want to cry.
A voice like yours so pure, so sweet, so high –
Where did you get it? You're so small and frail,
And yet you sing just like a nightingale."
"Thank you, my friend, although less well than you.
No bird of paradise sings better than you do."
"What awful nonsense both of you emote,"
Exclaimed a Sparrow, close at hand.
"When neither one of you can sing a note.
Why all this praise? I do not understand
(Since Rooster squawks and Cuckoo's always flat)
What game you think you're playing at."

If praise unearned you want, it's easy to obtain:
Just offer tit for tat – that's how you play this game.
Thus, Rooster praises Cuckoo, so she'll do the same.

Бритвы

С знакомцем съехавшись однажды я в дороге,
С ним вместе на одном ночлеге ночевал.
Поутру, чуть лишь я глаза продрал,
И что же узнаю? – Приятель мой в тревоге:
Вчера заснули мы меж шуток, без забот;
Теперь я слушаю – приятель стал не тот.
То вскрикнет он, то охнет, то вздохнёт.
"Что сделалось с тобой, мой милый?.. Я надеюсь,
Не болен ты". – "Ох! Ничего: я бреюсь". –
"Как! Только?" Тут я встал – гляжу: проказник мой
У зеркала сквозь слёз так кисло морщит рожу,
Как будто бы с него содрать сбирались кожу.
Узнавши, наконец, вину беды такой,
"Что дива? – я сказал; – ты сам себя тиранишь.
Пожалуй, посмотри:
Ведь у тебя не Бритвы-косари;
Не бриться – мучиться ты только с ними станешь". –
"Ох, братец, признаюсь,
Что Бритвы очень тупы!
Как этого не знать? Ведь мы не так уж глупы;
Да острыми – то я порезаться боюсь". –
"А я, мой друг, тебя уверить смею,
Что Бритвою тупой изрежешься скорей,
А острою обреешься верней:
Умей владеть лишь ею".

Вам пояснить рассказ мой я готов:
Не так ли многие, хоть стыдно им признаться,
С умом людей – боятся,
И терпят при себе охотней дураков?

The Razor

A friend and I once traveled far from home
And shared a room when stopping on the way.
One morning I awoke to greet the day
And from my friend I thought I heard a groan.
Last night he'd gone to bed content.
But now he seemed to suffer some torment.
Not only did he groan, he sighed and gasped and swore.
"My friend, what's wrong, what can I do?"
"Why not a thing! I'm shaving, nothing more."
I turned to look and found that this was true.
But from his grim expression it appeared
He was removing skin and not just beard.
And then I saw the reason, so I said,
"Your razor's only good for cutting bread.
Each day you suffer, curse and bleed,
And yet a whetstone's all you need."
"Of course. I know my razor's dull.
That's plain to see, I'm no numbskull.
But with a sharp one, I would fear,
I'd cut my throat from ear to ear."
"Old pal, just the reverse is true:
Dull razors are much worse for you.
A sharp one, once you've learned its use,
Will save your face from more abuse."

The hidden meaning of this tale I'll now impart:
Just like my friend there are some people who'll
From fear avoid companions deemed too smart
And tolerate instead someone who is a fool.

Крестьянин и Собака

У мужика, большого эконома,
Хозяина зажиточного дома,
Собака нанялась и двор стеречь,
И хлебы печь,
И сверх того полоть и поливать рассаду.
Какой же выдумал он вздор, –
Читатель говорит, – тут нет ни складу,
Ни ладу.
Пускай бы стеречи уж двор;
Да видано ль, чтоб где собаки хлеб пекали
Или рассаду поливали?
Читатель! Я бы был не прав кругом,
Когда сказал бы: "да", – да дело здесь не в том,
А в том, что наш Барбос за всё за это взялся,
И вымолвил себе он плату за троих;
Барбосу хорошо: что нужды до других.
Хозяин между тем на ярмарку собрался,
Поехал, погулял – приехал и назад,
Посмотрит – жизни стал не рад,
И рвёт, и мечет он с досады:
Ни хлеба дома, ни рассады.
А сверх того к нему на двор
Залез и клеть его обкрал начисто вор.
Вот на Барбоса тут посыпалось руганье;
Но у него на всё готово оправданье:
Он за рассадою печь хлеб никак не мог;
Рассадник оттого лишь только не удался,
Что, сторожа вокруг двора, он стал без ног;
А вора он затем не устерёг,
Что хлебы печь тогда сбирался.

The Peasant and the Dog

A peasant for his thrift admired,
A watchdog once had hired
To serve as guard
And tend the yard,
And bake the bread as well.
"What rot," I hear my readers yell.
"No dog could bake
Or water, much less rake.
You've picked a senseless tale to tell."
That is as it may be;
And yet the wages were so large
That greedy dog agreed.
The peasant left the dog in charge
And to a fair went he.
When he returned quite late that day,
He found the place in disarray.
No bread was baked; no dough was kneaded
The yard had not been raked, nor weeded.
And then the worst offense –
Some thieves had snuck unhindered through the fence.
The peasant, full of indignation,
Then heaped the dog with condemnation.
Anticipating such abuse,
The dog had readied his excuse:
He could not tend the yard
When he was standing guard;
Nor while engaged in raking,
Could he attend to baking;
And who, while baking bread,
Could chase off thieves instead?

Вельможа

Какой-то в древности Вельможа
С богато убранного ложа
Отправился в страну, где царствует Плутон.
Сказать простее, – умер он;
И так, как встарь велось, в аду на суд явился.
Тотчас допрос ему: “Чем был ты? где родился?” –
“Родился в Персии, а чином был сатрап;
Но так как, живучи, я был здоровьем слаб,
То сам я областью не правил,
А все дела секретарю оставил”. –
“Что ж делал ты?” – “Пил, ел и спал,
Да все подписывал, что он ни подавал”.
– “Скорей же в рай его!” – “Как! где же справедливость
Меркурий тут вскричал, забывши всю учтивость.
“Эх, братец! – отвечал Эак, –
Не знаешь дела ты никак.
Не видишь разве ты? Покойник – был дурак!
Что, если бы с такою властью
Взялся он за дела, к несчастью, –
Ведь погубил бы целый край!..
И ты б там слёз не обобрался!
Затем – то и попал он в рай,
Что за дела не принимался”.

Вчера я был в суде и видел там судью:
Ну, так и кажется, что быть ему в раю!

The VIP

In ancient times an ailing VIP
Rose from his bed of luxury
And traveled to Tsar Pluto's land.
I mean he'd died, you understand.
That country's surely no resort:
Our traveler had to face a court
Before they'd let him in.
Therein the judges asked his name,
From whence he came
And what his post had been.
"I ruled a Persian province for the king
But I felt ill and hardly did a thing.
I left the real work to my aide
And he's the one who all my rulings made."
"But all that time, what did you do?"
"Ate, drank and slept and signed a few
Official papers, all unread."
"To Paradise with him," the Chief Judge said.
Then someone cried, "I must object,
This man did nothing worth respect.
So why is he rewarded?"
The judge replied, "It's very plain
That you're new here, so I'll explain
Just why this verdict was accorded.
You surely see this man's a fool
And quite incapable of rule.
So if to rule his province he'd endeavored
It might have been destroyed forever.
To Paradise we send a few
As a reward for what they failed to do."

I have observed a judge or two of late
Who, I feel sure, will share my hero's fate.

Волк и Кот

Волк из лесу в деревню забежал,
Не в гости, но живот спасая;
За шкуру он свою дрожал:
Охотники за ним гнались и гончих стая.
Он рад бы в первые тут шмыгнуть ворота,
Да то лишь горе,
Что все ворота на запоре.
Вот видит Волк мой на заборе
Кота
И молит: "Васенька, мой друг! скажи скорее,
Кто здесь из мужичков добрее,
Чтобы укрыть меня от злых моих врагов?
Ты слышишь лай собак и страшный звук рогов!
Все это ведь за мной". – "Проси скорей Степана;
Мужик предобрый он", – Кот-Васька говорит.
"То так; да у него я ободрал барана". –
"Ну, попытайся ж у Демьяна". –
"Боюсь, что на меня и он сердит:
Я у него унёс козлёнка". –
"Беги ж, вон там живёт Трофим". –
"К Трофиму? Нет, боюсь и встретиться я с ним:
Он на меня с весны грозится за ягнёнка!" –
"Ну, плохо ж! – Но авось тебя укроет Клим!" –
"Ох, Вася, у него зарезал я телёнка!" –
"Что вижу, кум! Ты всем в деревне насолил, –
Сказал тут Васька Волку, –
Какую ж ты себе защиту здесь сулил?
Нет, в наших мужиках не столько мало толку,
Чтоб на свою беду тебя спасли они.
И правы, – сам себя вини:
Что ты посеял-то и жни".

The Wolf and the Cat

A Wolf came to a village, running at top speed,
In search of refuge, desperate in his need.
A group of hounds and hunters followed on his trail.
He trembled from his nose down to his bushy tail.
He gladly would have dived through any open gate,
But all were locked, as it was late.
Then he observed a Cat just sitting on a fence.
He spoke in gentle tones, so not to give offense,
"Oh, Tom, my friend! Please tell me if you can,
Which among your peasants is the nicest man?
Those shouts and barks you hear are hunters after me.
Who here might hide a Wolf from such an enemy?"
Tom Cat replied, "Try Steve, for he is very kind."
"No, I once killed his lamb; it may be on his mind."
"Well, then perhaps you might try Will."
"I mauled his goat; he bears me ill."
"Who else is there? I know – go talk to Paul.
He just may be the nicest one of all."
"No, that nice Paul would never do:
He's angry that I carried off his ewe."
"Oh, that's too bad: then I suggest old Clem."
"He hates me for his calves and what I did to them."
"Well, Wolf," said Tom, "I don't know what to say.
You've turned our folk against you; now you have to pay.
For none of them are fools enough to shelter you.
They still remember each dead calf and ewe.
What shepherd would help save a Wolf who'd killed his sheep?
My friend, what you have sown, now you will have to reap."

Филин и Осёл

Слепой Осёл в лесу с дороги сбился
(Он в дальний путь было пустился).
Но к ночи в чащу так забрёл мой сумасброд,
Что двинуться не мог ни взад он, ни вперёд.
И зрячему бы тут не выйти из хлопот,
Но Филин вблизости, по счастию, случился
И взялся быть Ослу проводником.
Все знают, Филины как ночью зорки:
Стремнины, рвы, бугры, пригорки,
Всё это различал мой Филин будто днём
И к утру выбрался на ровный путь с Ослом.
Ну, как с проводником таким расстаться?
Вот просит Филина Осёл, чтоб с ним остаться,
И вздумал изойти он с Филином весь свет.
Мой Филин господином
Уселся на хребте Ослином,
И стали путь держать, счастливо ль только?
Нет:
Лишь солнце на небе поутру заиграло,
У Филина в глазах темнее ночи стало.
Однако ж Филин мой упрям;
Ослу советует и вкось и впрям.
“Остерегись! – кричит, – направо будем в луже”.
Но лужи не было, а влево вышло хуже.
“Ещё левей возьми, ещё левее шаг!”
И – бух Осёл, и с Филином, в овраг.

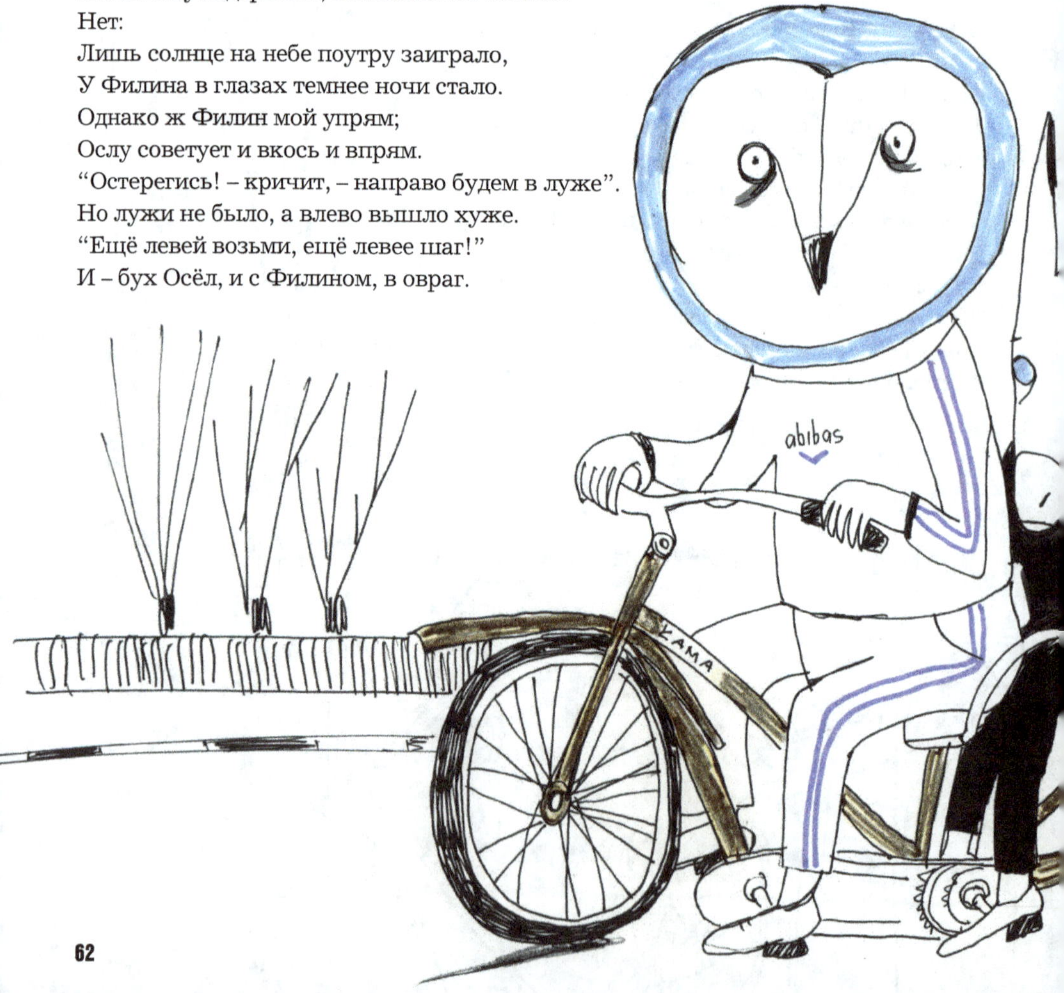

The Owl and the Ass

A blind Jackass soon lost his way
While traveling through the woods one day.
By nightfall he was stuck in brush so thick
He could not move, whichever way he picked.
Indeed, a man or beast with sight
Could not have found the road that night.
But Fortune smiled: an Owl lived nearby,
And was attracted by the Ass's desperate cry.
And since he had a heart both big and good,
He undertook to guide Ass from the wood.
Now, owls see at night like others do by day.
From ditches, knolls, and such he steered the Ass away
And got him on a level track by break of day.
The grateful Ass was loath to part from his good guide
And begged him not to go and offered him a ride.
So Owl clambered up on Ass's back
And both of them set out upon the track.
"A happy ending," some of you might say.
No way!
With morning light surrounding him,
The Owl's eyes began to dim.
No longer could he see to guide.
But Owls have their share of pride
And like to lead the way at any price,
So he kept on with his advice.
"Go left, no, no, it's right I mean."
And crash! They fell in a ravine.

Белка

У Льва служила Белка.
Не знаю, как и чем; но дело только в том,
Что служба Белкина угодна перед Львом;
А угодить на Льва, конечно, не безделка.
За то обещан ей орехов целый воз.
Обещан – между тем всё время улетает;
А Белочка моя нередко голодает
И скалит перед Львом зубки свои сквозь слёз
Посмотрит: по лесу то там, то сям мелькают
Её подружки в вышине;
Она лишь глазками моргает, а оне
Орешки, знай себе, щелкают да щелкают.
Но наша Белочка к орешнику лишь шаг,
Глядит – нельзя никак:
На службу Льву её то кличут, то толкают.
Вот Белка, наконец, уж стала и стара
И Льву наскучила: в отставку ей пора.
Отставку Белке дали,
И точно, целый воз орехов ей прислали.
Орехи славные, каких не видел свет;
Все на отбор: орех к ореху – чудо!
Одно лишь только худо –
Давно зубов у Белки нет.

The Squirrel

Once a Squirrel served King Lion well.
Just what her service was I cannot tell,
But what's important's that it pleased the King,
Which, as all know, is no small thing.
The Lion, in his gratitude and pleasure,
Declared he would reward her with a treasure –
A lifetime's worth of nuts – enough to fill a cart.
Of course, this warmed the Squirrel's heart.
Yet time went by and still no walnuts came;
And Squirrel's belly often burned with hunger's flame.
Meanwhile her friends within the wood
Consumed as many nuts as squirrels could.
But when she managed to escape from court
And found and climbed a prime nut tree,
Her time there always was cut short,
For she was sent for urgently,
To do some thing the King required.
With time she grew too old and tired
To do the tasks for which she had been hired.
And so he ordered her to be retired
With honors. Then at last the nuts were sent –
The choicest nuts, in fullest complement –
A great and regal gesture, without doubt.
And yet, our Squirrel's teeth had long since fallen out.

Волк и Журавль

Что волки жадны, всякий знает:
Волк, евши, никогда
Костей не разбирает.
За то на одного из них пришла беда:
Он костью чуть не подавился.
Не может Волк ни охнуть, ни вздохнуть;
Пришло хоть ноги протянуть!
По счастью, близко тут Журавль случился.
Вот кой – как знаками стал Волк его манить
И просит горю пособить.
Журавль свой нос по шею
Засунул к Волку в пасть и с трудностью большею
Кость вытащил и стал за труд просить.
"Ты шутишь! – зверь вскричал коварный, –
Тебе за труд? Ах ты, неблагодарный!
А это ничего, что свой ты долгий нос
И с глупой головой из горла цел унёс!
Поди ж, приятель, убирайся,
Да берегись: вперёд ты мне не попадайся".

The Wolf and the Crane

Now wolves are noted for their greed,
And swallow bones each time they feed.
One Wolf had cause to rue this greedy habit:
A bone stuck in his throat (perhaps from some poor rabbit).
He could not speak, nor howl, nor even sigh,
And felt quite sure he was about to die.
But luckily a Crane was passing by.
The Wolf, by gesturing and painful yelp,
Implored the Crane to try to help.
Although Wolf's teeth caused Crane to shake with dread,
Into Wolf's throat he plunged his beak and head.
The bone refused to budge – stuck fast.
He pulled and pulled and got it out at last.
Then meekly asked for a reward.
At this the Wolf, his voice recovered, roared,
"Reward? What nerve! You should thank me in fact!
For I returned your head and neck intact!
I almost never am so kind.
Begone, before I change my mind."

Муха и Пчела

В саду, весной, при легком ветерке,
На тонком стебельке
Качалась Муха, сидя,
И на цветке Пчелу увидя,
Спесиво говорит: “Уж как тебе не лень
С утра до вечера трудиться целый день!
На месте бы твоём я в сутки захирела.
Вот, например, моё
Так, право, райское житьё!
За мною только лишь и дела:
Летать по балам, по гостям:
И молвить, не хвалясь, мне в городе знакомы
Вельмож и богачей все домы.
Когда б ты видела, как я пирую там!
Где только свадьба, именины, –
Из первых я уж верно тут.
И ем с фарфоровых богатых блюд,
И пью из хрусталей блестящих сладки вины,
И прежде всех гостей
Беру, что вздумаю, из лакомых сластей;
Притом же, жалуя пол нежной,
Вкруг молодых красавиц вьюсь
И отдыхать у них сажусь
На щёчке розовой иль шейке белоснежной”. –
“Всё это знаю я, – ответствует Пчела. –
Но и о том дошли мне слухи,
Что никому ты не мила,
Что на пирах лишь морщатся от Мухи,
Что даже часто, где покажешься ты в дом,
Тебя гоняют со стыдом”. –
“Вот, – Муха говорит, – гоняют! Что ж такое?
Коль выгонят в окно, так я влечу в другое”.

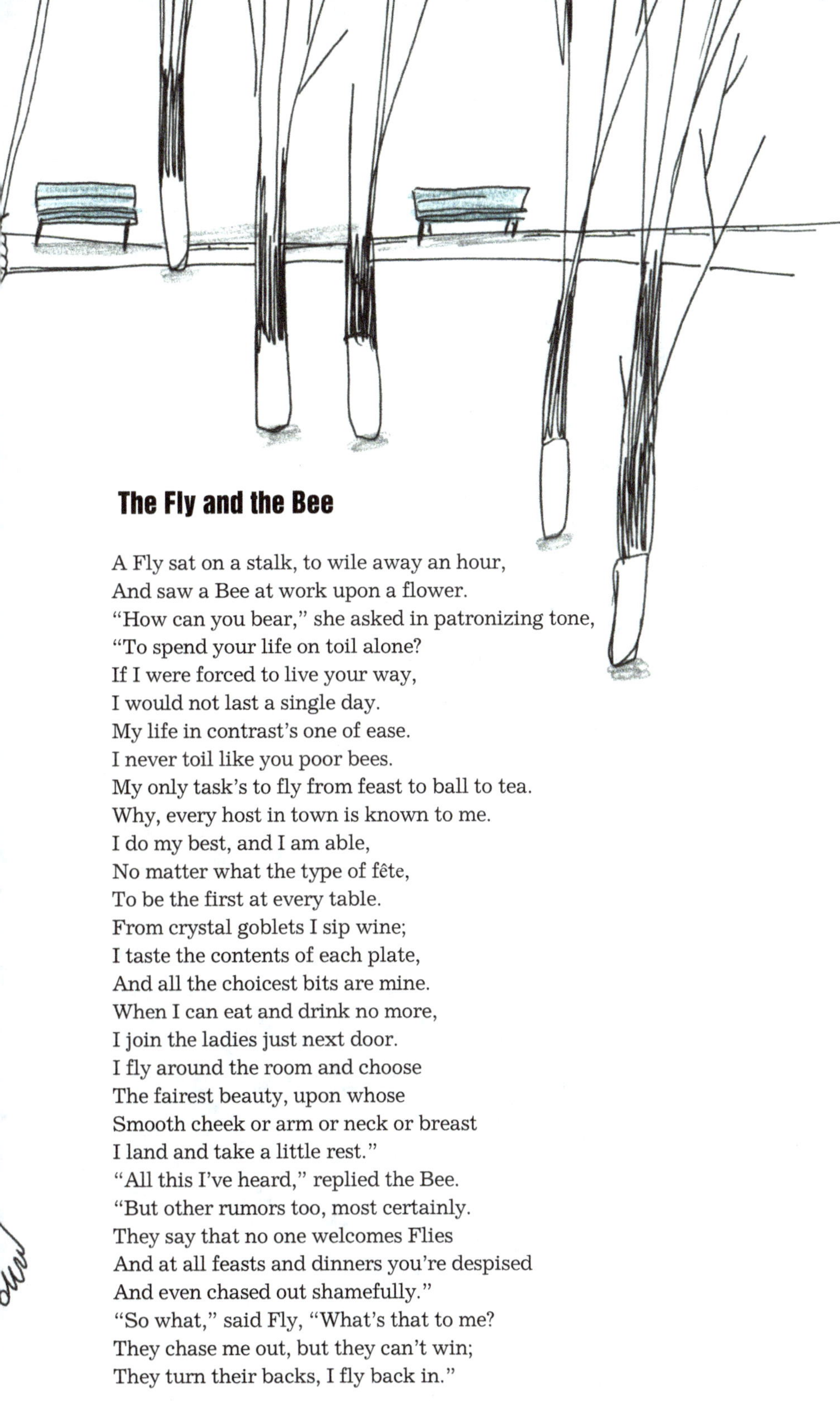

The Fly and the Bee

A Fly sat on a stalk, to wile away an hour,
And saw a Bee at work upon a flower.
"How can you bear," she asked in patronizing tone,
"To spend your life on toil alone?
If I were forced to live your way,
I would not last a single day.
My life in contrast's one of ease.
I never toil like you poor bees.
My only task's to fly from feast to ball to tea.
Why, every host in town is known to me.
I do my best, and I am able,
No matter what the type of fête,
To be the first at every table.
From crystal goblets I sip wine;
I taste the contents of each plate,
And all the choicest bits are mine.
When I can eat and drink no more,
I join the ladies just next door.
I fly around the room and choose
The fairest beauty, upon whose
Smooth cheek or arm or neck or breast
I land and take a little rest."
"All this I've heard," replied the Bee.
"But other rumors too, most certainly.
They say that no one welcomes Flies
And at all feasts and dinners you're despised
And even chased out shamefully."
"So what," said Fly, "What's that to me?
They chase me out, but they can't win;
They turn their backs, I fly back in."

Комар и Пастух

Пастух под тенью спал, надеяся на псов.
Приметя то, змея из-под кустов
Ползёт к нему, вон высунувши жало;
И Пастуха на свете бы не стало,
Но, сжаляся над ним, Комар, что было сил,
Сонливца укусил.
Проснувшися, Пастух змею убил;
Но прежде Комара спросонья так хватил,
Что бедного его как не бывало.

Таких примеров есть немало:
Коль слабый сильному, хоть движимый добром.
Открыть глаза на правду покусится,
Того и жди, что то же с ним случится,
Что с Комаром.

The Mosquito and the Shepherd

A Shepherd left the dogs to tend his sheep.
Then found a shady spot and went to sleep.
A serpent saw him undefended
And slithered toward him, fangs extended.
But a Mosquito, very kind of heart,
Observed all this and did his part –
He bit the sleeper hard,
Which caused the shepherd to awake
And spy and kill the snake.
But first he'd smashed the insect on his skin,
Who was no more – as if he'd never been.

You must exert the greatest care
In warning big shots to beware.
If you're a man of low estate,
You're apt to share Mosquito's fate.

Туча

Над изнуренною от зноя стороною
Большая Туча пронеслась;
Ни каплею её не освежа одною,
Она большим дождем над морем пролилась
И щедростью своей хвалилась пред Горою.
“Что сделала добра
Ты щедростью такою? –
Сказала ей Гора. –
И как смотреть на то не больно!
Когда бы на поля свой дождь ты пролила,
Ты б область целую от голода спасла:
А в море без тебя, мой друг, воды довольно”.

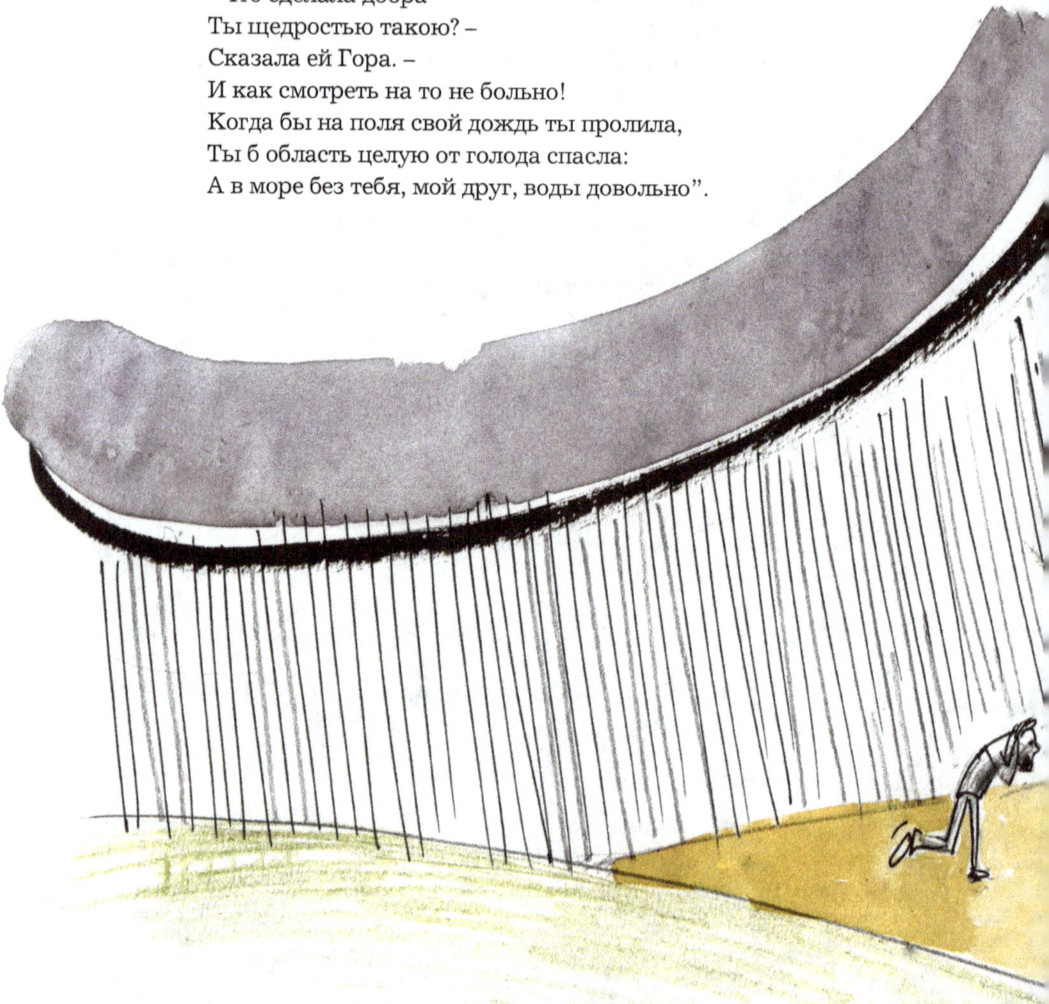

The Storm Cloud

A rain cloud passed above a dried-out land,
But did not spill a drop to lend a hand.
Instead, she poured her bounty on the sea
Then boasted of her generosity.
A Mountain overheard and said:
"Although you gave your water freely,
What good do gifts like yours do, really?
Now, if to that parched land instead
Your rain had been diverted,
A famine would have been averted.
If I gave water to the sea,
I would not boast of generosity."

Котёнок и Скворец

В каком-то доме был Скворец,
Плохой певец;
Зато уж философ презнатный,
И свел с Котёнком дружбу он.
Котёнок был уж котик преизрядный,
Но тих, и вежлив, и смирён.
Вот как-то был в столе Котёнок обделён.
Бедняжку голод мучит:
Задумчив бродит он, скучаючи постом;
Поводит ласково хвостом
И жалобно мяучит.
А философ Котёнка учит
И говорит ему: "Мой друг, ты очень прост,
Что терпишь добровольно пост;
А в клетке над носом твоим висит щеглёнок:
Я вижу, ты прямой Котёнок". –
"Но совесть..." – "Как ты мало знаешь свет!
Поверь, что это сущий бред
И слабых душ одни лишь предрассудки,
А для больших умов – пустые только шутки!
На свете кто силён,
Тот делать всё волён.
Вот доказательства тебе и вот примеры". –
Тут, выведя их на свои манеры,
Он философию всю вычерпал до дна.
Котёнку натощак понравилась она:
Он вытащил и съел щеглёнка.
Разлакомил кусок такой Котёнка,
Хотя им голода он утолить не мог.
Однако же второй урок
С большим успехом слушал
И говорит Скворцу: "Спасибо, милый кум!
Наставил ты меня на ум".
И, клетку разломав, учителя он скушал.

The Kitten and the Starling

Some people kept a Starling in a cage
Who thought himself philosopher and sage.
(An image that perhaps he cultivated
Because his singing was so denigrated.)
Now sages need disciples, so it's written.
For his, the Starling chose his master's Kitten,
Who, though he had an eager intellect,
Was meek and showed his mentor much respect.
One day, by some mishap, the Kitten got no food.
But, to protest, he merely sadly mewed.
Outraged the Starling lectured him,
"To take this lying down, you must be awfully dim,
When over there's a finch, our master's useless pet,
She sings quite well; and tastes good too, I'd bet."
"Eat up the finch. But that is wrong."
"Just for the weak, but not the strong.
My little friend, you're still naive.
Now, we philosophers believe
That those who dare can break the rules,
While those who don't are spineless fools."
The Kitten, sharp in mind and likewise tooth,
Was sure his mentor always spoke the truth.
He snatched the finch and ruthlessly he ate it.
It tasted good, but left him less than sated.
And though with hunger still his belly burned,
He thanked his mentor for the lesson learned.
And then he took the Starling at his word
And caught and ate his second bird.

Лисица и Сурок

“Куда так, кумушка, бежишь ты без оглядки?” –
Лисицу спрашивал Сурок.
“Ох, мой голубчик-куманёк!
Терплю напраслину и выслана за взятки.
Ты знаешь, я была в курятнике судьёй,
Утратила в делах здоровье и покой,
В трудах куска недоедала,
Ночей недосыпала:
И я ж за то под гнев подпала;
А всё по клеветам. Ну, сам подумай ты:
Кто ж будет в мире прав, коль слушать клеветы?
Мне взятки брать? да разве я взбешуся!
Ну, видывал ли ты, я на тебя пошлюся,
Чтоб этому была причастна я греху?
Подумай, вспомни хорошенько”. –
“Нет, кумушка; а видывал частенько,
Что рыльце у тебя в пуху”.

Иной при месте так вздыхает,
Как будто рубль последний доживает:
И подлинно, весь город знает,
Что у него ни за собой,
Ни за женой, –
А смотришь, помаленьку
То домик выстроит, то купит деревеньку.
Теперь, как у него приход с расходом свесть,
Хоть по суду и не докажешь,
Но как не согрешишь, не скажешь:
Что у него пушок на рыльце есть.

The Vixen and the Woodchuck

A Woodchuck spied a Vixen running by
And called, "My dear, what is your hurry?
You've never been in such a flurry."
"They're after me," came her reply.
"I have been slandered and exiled.
My spotless honor's been defiled.
They say that I've misused my post
As henhouse viceroy. It's the most
Unfounded charge I ever heard.
I took no bribe from any bird,
But sacrificed both food and rest
For those fool hens. I did my best.
But with false slander and vile smear,
They have destroyed my life's career.
Dear Woodchuck, we've been friends so long.
When have you known me to do wrong:
Accepting bribes, inviting graft?"
The Woodchuck looked at her and laughed.
"Oh, no, I've never seen you sin,
But I've seen feathers on your chin."

Some public servants moan and sigh,
Complain they're barely getting by.
Indeed in town it is well known
They have no fortunes of their own.
And yet from year to year we see
Them growing richer gradually,
Beyond their modest salary.
And though hard evidence is slim
We'd have to say (to lie's a sin)
They too have feathers on their chin.

Лев и Мышь

У Льва просила Мышь смиренно позволенья
Поблизости его в дупле завесть селенье
И так примолвила: “Хотя-де здесь, в лесах,
Ты и могуч и славен;
Хоть в силе Льву никто не равен
И рёв один его на всех наводит страх,
Но будущее кто угадывать возьмётся –
Как знать? кому в ком нужда доведётся?
И как я ни мала кажусь,
А, может быть, подчас тебе и пригожусь”. –
“Ты! – вскрикнул Лев. – Ты, жалкое созданье!
За эти дерзкие слова
Ты стоишь смерти в наказанье.
Прочь, прочь отсель, пока жива –
Иль твоего не будет праху”.
Тут Мышка бедная, не вспомнясь от страху,
Со всех пустилась ног – простыл её и след.
Льву даром не прошла, однако ж, гордость эта:
Отправяся искать добычи на обед,
Попался он в тенета.
Без пользы сила в нём, напрасен рёв и стон,
Как он ни рвался, ни метался,
Но всё добычею охотника остался,
И в клетке на показ народу увезён.
Про Мышку бедную тут поздно вспомнил он,
Что бы помочь она ему сумела,
Что сеть бы от её зубов не уцелела
И что его своя кичливость съела.

Читатель, истину любя,
Примолвлю к басне я, и то не от себя –
Не попусту в народе говорится:
Не плюй в колодезь, пригодится
Воды напиться.

The Lion and the Mouse

A perfect nest site for a Mouse
Was right next door to Lion's house.
So Mouse, a meek and timid thing,
Politely asked the Lion King
For royal permission to move there.
"Please let me live next to your lair.
You're great and mighty; I am small,
But if I moved here, still and all,
Some day I just might be of use."
At this the Lion heaped abuse
Upon the Mouse. "How dare you show such disrespect?
You piddling creature, you insect.
I'll take your head off with one bite.
If you would live, flee from my sight!"
The Mouse ran off – half dead with fear.
She found a new site for her den
And never showed up there again.
But Lion for his pride paid dear:
While he was hunting, free from care,
A hunter's net got him ensnared.
He struggled, thrashed, his muscles strained,
And yet, despite his might and mane,
Caught in the net he still remained.
All he could do was roar in pain
At his plight as hunters' prey.
(It served him right, some folks might say.)
They caged him up that very day
And made of him a zoo display.
He soon recalled the lowly Mouse.
If she had settled near his house,
She would have come, a friend in need,
Chewed through the net; he'd have been freed.
He spent his days in penitence,
Regretting his past arrogance.

Our people have a saying I would share with you
Dear reader, mark it well, for it is true.
Ere spitting in a well, you'd better stop to think
That there may come a day you'll need to take a drink.

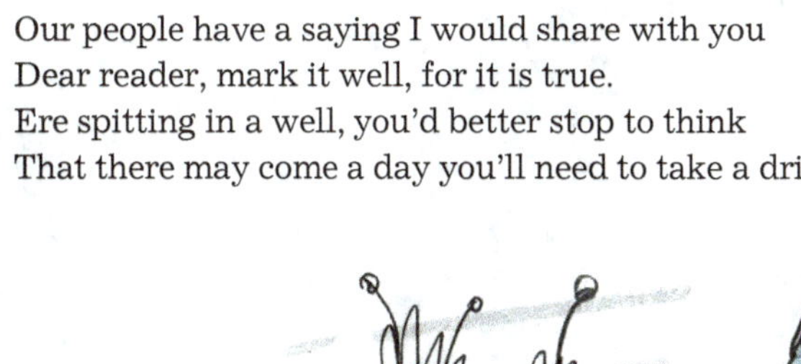

Стрекоза и Муравей

Попрыгунья Стрекоза
Лето красное пропела;
Оглянуться не успела,
Как зима катит в глаза.
Помертвело чисто поле;
Нет уж дней тех светлых боле,
Как под каждым ей листком
Был готов и стол, и дом.
Всё прошло: с зимой холодной
Нужда, голод настаёт;
Стрекоза уж не поёт:
И кому же в ум пойдёт
На желудок петь голодный!
Злой тоской удручена,
К Муравью ползёт она:
"Не оставь меня, кум милой!
Дай ты мне собраться с силой
И до вешних только дней
Прокорми и обогрей!" –
"Кумушка, мне странно это:
Да работала ль ты в лето?" –
Говорит ей Муравей.
"До того ль, голубчик, было?
В мягких муравах у нас –
Песни, резвость всякий час,
Так что голову вскружило". –
"А, так ты..." – "Я без души
Лето целое всё пела". –
"Ты всё пела? Это дело:
Так поди же, попляши!"

The Dragonfly and the Ants

The flighty feckless Dragonfly
Sang songs as summer days flew by.
Before she'd time to turn around,
The leaves had fallen on the ground,
And everything was dead or dying.
Those days were gone when, without trying,
Beneath each leaf more food she found,
And shelter too. Such times had passed,
Replaced by winter's icy fast.
Then Dragonfly felt hunger's pang
And, no surprise, no longer sang.
At last, depressed and in despair, our Dragonfly decided
To look for refuge at the hill where ants resided.
And spotting some she knew, she pled,
"Take pity on me; I'm half dead.
Your hill is warm; you've food to spare.
You've had good fortune. Why not share?
Please save my life and let me stay
Until the spring, at most till May."
The Ants, perplexed, asked of their neighbor,
"How could you let things get this way?
Was not your summer spent in labor?"
"No, it was not, please understand
Each balmy day our merry band
Of flies disported in the grass.
I lived a life of play and song
And never once, all summer long,
Remembered that I must amass
A store of food, alas!"
"You mean to say that you..."
"That's right, I sang all summer through,
And left the winter up to chance."
"Well then, perhaps what you should do,"
Replied the Ants,
"Is dance."

Собака и Лошадь

У одного крестьянина служа,
Собака с Лошадью считаться как – то стали.
“Вот, – говорит Барбос, – большая госпожа!
По мне хоть бы тебя совсем с двора согнали.
Велика вещь возить или пахать!
Об удальстве твоём другого не слыхать:
И можно ли тебе равняться в чём со мною?
Ни днём, ни ночью я не ведаю покою:
Днём стадо под моим надзором на лугу,
А ночью дом я стерегу”. –
“Конечно, – Лошадь отвечала, –
Твоя правдива речь;
Однако же, когда б я не пахала,
То нечего б тебе здесь было и стеречь”.

The Dog and the Horse

A peasant had two servants – Dog and Horse.
Dog felt himself superior, of course,
And told the Horse he was of little worth.
"You're no big deal, with me you can't compete;
Your labor isn't worth the hay you eat.
Why, any fool could pull a cart and plow the earth.
It takes no courage; you're not stressed.
But me, why, night and day I never rest.
I guard the flock all day, at night the house and yard!"
"There's truth in what you say, I must allow,"
Said Horse, "Your work is dangerous and hard.
Yet, if I didn't plow,
What would there be to guard?"

Крестьяне и Река

Крестьяне, вышед из терпенья
От разоренья,
Что речки им и ручейки
При водополье причиняли,
Пошли просить себе управы у Реки,
В которую ручьи и речки те впадали.
И было что на них донесть!
Где озими разрыты;
Где мельницы посорваны и смыты;
Потоплено скота, что и не счесть!
А та Река течёт так смирно, хоть и пышно;
На ней стоят большие города,
И никогда
За ней таких проказ не слышно:
Так, верно, их она уймёт,
Между собой Крестьяне рассуждали.
Но что ж? как подходить к Реке поближе стали
И посмотрели, так узнали,
Что половину их добра по ней несёт.
Тут, попусту не заводя хлопот,
Крестьяне лишь его глазами проводили;
Потом взглянулись меж собой
И, покачавши головой,
Пошли домой.
А отходя, проговорили:
“На что и время тратить нам!
На младших не найдёшь себе управы там,
Где делятся они со старшим пополам”.

The Farmers and the River

A certain plain had many farms and ranches,
But also many flood-prone river branches.
And, every spring or so,
All these would overflow.
So stock and mills and crops were lost,
For which the Farmers paid the cost.
Fed up and full of indignation
At damage from this inundation,
And hoping for just compensation,
The Farmers sent a delegation
To see the major River on the plain.
"Though by our branches she is fed,
This River never floods," they said.
"If of her branches we complain,
Of course, she'll make them quit."
They felt quite sure of it,
Until they got there and could see
The River had their property,
Which floated downstream merrily.
The peasants shook their heads and frowned
And then they turned around
For home. They knew complaints are of no use
When smart abusers pay their dues
And share ill-gotten plunder
With those they serve under.

Орёл и Пчела

Счастлив, кто на чреде трудится знаменитой:
Ему и то уж силы придаёт,
Что подвигов его свидетель целый свет.
Но сколь и тот почтен, кто, в низости сокрытый,
За все труды, за весь потерянный покой
Ни славою, ни почестьми не льстится,
И мыслью оживлён одной:
Что к пользе общей он трудится.

Увидя, как Пчела хлопочет вкруг цветка,
Сказал Орёл однажды ей с презреньем:
“Как ты, бедняжка, мне жалка,
Со всей твоей работой и с уменьем!
Вас в улье тысячи всё лето лепят сот:
Да кто же после разберёт
И отличит твои работы?
Я, право, не пойму охоты:
Трудиться целый век и что ж иметь в виду?..
Безвестной умереть со всеми наряду!
Какая разница меж нами!
Когда, расширяся шумящими крылами,
Ношуся я под облаками,
То всюду рассеваю страх:
Не смеют от земли пернатые подняться,
Не дремлют пастухи при тучных их стадах;
Ни лани быстрые не смеют на полях,
Меня завидя, показаться”.
Пчела ответствует: “Тебе хвала и честь!
Да продлит над тобой Зевес свои щедроты!
А я, родясь труды для общей пользы несть,
Не отличать ищу свои работы,
Но утешаюсь тем, на наши смотря соты,
Что в них и моего хоть капля мёду есть”.

The Eagle and the Bee

Most fortunate is he who's earned his fame
From exploits that do honor to his name,
For he draws power from the world's acclaim.
But just as worthy of respect are those, unknown,
Who toil to serve the common good and not their own.
They fame and riches neither seek nor find,
Their sole reward's the thought that they have helped mankind.

An Eagle watched a toiling Bee
Abuzz around a rose
And spoke to her with courtesy
(Though looking down his nose).
"I'm sorry for you, my poor bee.
You work so hard with such ability,
But thousands from the hive that is your home
All work just as you do to build the honeycomb.
Yet, after it is built no one can tell
Which bee did what, whose work is in which cell.
I do not understand how this can satisfy –
To labor in a swarm and then, without distinction, die!
How different from you bees am I!
I always stand out from the crowds.
When I take flight into the clouds,
The beasts below are filled with fear.
Small birds and creatures, timid deer
All hide themselves when I appear.
And men who see me in the sky
Look on in awe and yearn to fly."
Bee said, "Your fame you well deserve.
May Zeus prolong your days of glory.
The life I lead's a different story,
For bees like me are born to serve.
Our honey goes into a common store.
Which drops are mine I cannot tell;
But when I see our comb with honey in each cell
I know that mine are there, and do not wish for more."

Скупой и Курица

Скупой теряет всё, желая всё достать.
Чтоб долго мне примеров не искать,
Хоть есть и много их, я в том уверен;
Да рыться лень: так я намерен
Вам басню старую сказать.

Вот что в ребячестве читал я про Скупого.
Был человек, который никакого
Не знал ни промысла, ни ремесла,
Но сундуки его полнели очевидно.
Он Курицу имел (как это не завидно!),
Котора яйца несла,
Но не простые,
А золотые.
Иной бы тому был рад,
Что понемногу он становится богат;
Но этого Скупому мало,
Ему на мысли вспало,
Что, взрезав Курицу, он в ней достанет клад.
И так, забыв её к себе благодеянье,
Неблагодарности не побоясь греха,
Её зарезал он. И что же? В воздаянье
Он вынул из неё простые потроха.

The Greedy Man and the Hen

Although they have enough, the greedy strive for more.
They often thereby lose what wealth they have in store.
Examples of this truth are all around,
Although the best of these I've ever found
Comes from a fable told in days of yore.

There was a man who had no skill or trade with which
To earn his bread; and yet he had grown rich.
And each new day his riches grew again.
His secret? Well, he had a hen
Who laid him eggs of purest gold.
Now, this would fill most other men
With happiness untold.
But not this one, oh, no!
He thought one golden egg a day was much too slow
A rate to have his riches grow.
He felt no gratitude, though much was owed,
But used his knife to reach the mother lode
Of gold within his pet.
But though he butchered her no treasure did he get.
Inside she was a normal chicken from a coop,
With innards that were fit for just one thing – a soup.
And so she lost her life for naught, his wondrous hen,
And soon her owner had to toil, like other men.

Кошка и Соловей

В бедняжку когти запустила
И, ласково его сжимая, говорила:
"Соловушка, душа моя!
Я слышу, что тебя везде за песни славят
И с лучшими певцами рядом ставят.
Мне говорит лиса – кума,
Что голос у тебя так звонок и чудесен,
Что от твоих прелестных песен
Все пастухи, пастушки – без ума.
Хотела б очень я сама
Тебя послушать.
Не трепещися так; не будь, мой друг, упрям;
Не бойся: не хочу совсем тебя я кушать.
Лишь спой мне что – нибудь: тебе я волю дам
И отпущу гулять по рощам и лесам.
В любви я к музыке тебе не уступаю.
И часто, про себя мурлыча, засыпаю".
Меж тем мой бедный Соловей
Едва – едва дышал в когтях у ней.
"Ну, что же? – продолжает Кошка, –
Пропой, дружок, хотя немножко".
Но наш певец не пел, а только что пищал.
"Так этим – то леса ты восхищал! –
С насмешкою она спросила. –
Где ж эта чистота и сила,
О коих все без умолку твердят?
Мне скучен писк такой и от моих котят.
Нет, вижу, что в пенье ты вовсе не искусен:
Всё без начала, без конца.
Посмотрим, на зубах каков – то будешь вкусен!"
И съела бедного певца –
До крошки.

Сказать ли на ушко, яснее, мысль мою?
Худые песни Соловью
В когтях у Кошки.

The Cat and the Nightingale

A Cat once caught a Nightingale,
Who struggled in her claws – to no avail.
The Cat then clasped him close and whispered in his ear,
"Oh, Little Nightingale, my dear!
You know you are a famous bird.
All deem your voice the best they've ever heard –
So strong, so pure, so sweet,
That music lovers all are at your feet.
And all the wood has heard your lovely song,
Except for me. And, I confess, I long
To hear it too.
And so I've captured you
To hear you sing and not to eat.
As soon as you have sung a while for me,
My spirit soothed, I vow, I'll set you free.
Oh, do not tremble so, my sweet.
Just charm me with your songs and, at the least,
You'll find I'm really not a savage beast.
I am a music lover, just like you,
And often hum (or purr) the whole day through."
The Nightingale, too scared to sing or speak,
Still tried his best but managed just a squeak.
"Is this the voice that they all rave about?"
The Cat said with a sneer,
"The voice so pure and sweet without
A single flaw, without a peer.
The squeaks my kittens make I cannot bear to hear,
And yours are just as bad, I fear.
My squeaky friend, your last song has been sung.
Though you've not pleased my ear,
Perhaps you'll please my tongue."
Then she devoured him in seconds flat.

The moral here? It's simply that
You can't expect to hear sweet songs
From birds trapped where no bird belongs –
Within the clutches of a Cat.

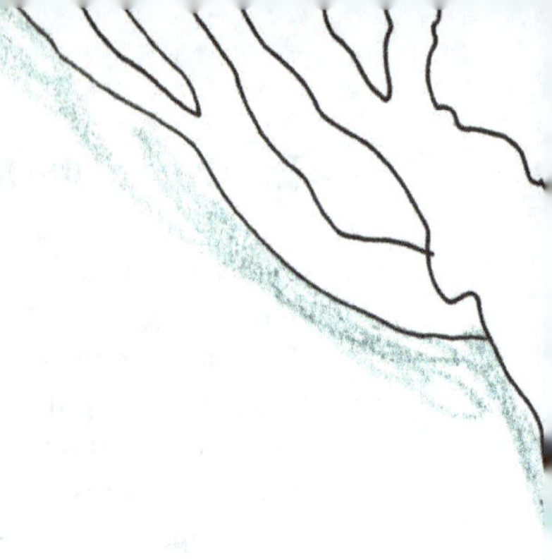

Дуб и Трость

С Тростинкой Дуб однажды в речь вошёл.
“Поистине, роптать ты вправе на природу, –
Сказал он, – воробей, и тот тебе тяжёл.
Чуть лёгкий ветерок подёрнет рябью воду,
Ты зашатаешься, начнёшь слабеть
И так нагнёшься сиротливо,
Что жалко на тебя смотреть.
Меж тем как, наравне с Кавказом, горделиво,
Не только солнца я препятствую лучам,
Но, посмеваяся и вихрям и грозам,
Стою и твёрд и прям,
Как будто б ограждён ненарушимым миром.
Тебе всё бурей – мне всё кажется зефиром.
Хотя б уж ты в окружности росла,
Густою тенью ветвей моих покрытой,
От непогод бы я быть мог тебе защитой;
Но вам в удел природа отвела
Брега бурливого Эолова владенья:
Конечно, нет совсем у ней о вас раденья”. –
“Ты очень жалостлив, – сказала Трость в ответ, –
Однако не крушись: мне столько худа нет.
Не за себя я вихрей опасаюсь;
Хоть я и гнусь, но не ломаюсь:
Так бури мало мне вредят;
Едва ль не более тебе они грозят!
То правда, что ещё доселе их свирепость
Твою не одолела крепость
И от ударов их ты не склонял лица;
Но – подождём конца!”
Едва лишь это Трость сказала,
Вдруг мчится с северных сторон
И с градом и с дождём шумящий аквилон.
Дуб держится, – к земле Тростиночка припала.
Бушует ветр, удвоил силы он,
Взревел – и вырвал с корнем вон
Того, кто небесам главой своей касался
И в области теней пятою упирался.

The Oak and the Reed

One day an Oak said to a Reed, his friend,
"You've every right against your lot to rail.
A sparrow's tiny weight can make you bend.
And at the slightest breeze, you are so frail,
You quake and flounder to and fro.
Your head droops down so pitifully low
That I, for one, can scarcely bear to see.
If only you'd been born an Oak like me,
The equal of the mountains – tall, stalwart and proud.
At storms and thunder, I just laugh aloud.
The sun's own rays, no matter how intense,
Can't penetrate my leafy dense defense.
A wind I'd scarcely feel would toss you helter-skelter.
If only we'd been planted close together,
My presence would have given you some shelter
To shield you from the most destructive weather.
But Mother Nature's placed you far away
Upon the stormy shore of yonder bay.
She seems to care but little for your fate."
"All your concern I do appreciate,"
Politely said the Reed.
"Although in truth, for pity there's no need.
I'm not afraid of storms. Make no mistake,
Though I may sway and bend, I never break.
So do not give another thought to me.
Indeed, the danger's greater for a tree.
It's true, till now, when gales have raged and blown,
You've stood erect and not been overthrown,
Or even bent a bit beneath their blows.
But for the future, no one ever knows."
Just then there came a mighty hurricane
And lashed the land with awful winds and rain.
The Oak remained erect; the Reed bent to the ground.
The wind increased in force and with a crashing sound
The Oak, who proudly all the elements defied,
Uprooted, fell to earth, and died.

Лиса

Зимой, ранёхонько, близ жила,
Лиса у проруби пила в большой мороз.
Меж тем оплошность ли, судьба ль (не в этом сила),
Но – кончик хвостика Лисица замочила,
И ко льду он примёрз.
Беда не велика, легко б её поправить:
Рвануться только посильней
И волосков хотя десятка два оставить,
Но до людей
Домой убраться поскорей.
Да как испортить хвост? А хвост такой пушистый,
Раскидистый и золотистый!
Нет, лучше подождать – ведь спит ещё народ;
А между тем авось и оттепель придёт,
Так хвост от проруби оттает.
Вот ждёт – пождёт, а хвост лишь боле примерзает.
Глядит – и день светает,
Народ шевелится, и слышны голоса.
Тут бедная моя Лиса
Туда – сюда метаться;
Но уж от проруби не может оторваться.
По счастью, Волк бежит. “Друг милый! кум! отец! –
Кричит Лиса. – Спаси! Пришёл совсем конец!”
Вот кум остановился –
И в спасенье Лисы вступился.
Приём его был очень прост:
Он начисто отгрыз ей хвост.
Тут без хвоста домой моя пустилась дура.
Уж рада, что на ней цела осталась шкура.

Мне кажется, что смысл не тёмен басни сей:
Щепотки волосков Лиса не пожалей –
Остался б хвост у ней.

The Fox

At dawn a thirsty Fox stopped at a frozen lake.
(An ice hole there held water she could sip.)
But, carelessly, she made a big mistake,
And wet her tail, well, just the tip.
But still it quickly froze into the ice.
Now, all she had to do was tug it once or twice
And she'd be home before the nearby village stirred
At cost of but a meager sacrifice –
A small amount of hair.
To grudge this loss to me seems quite absurd.
And yet she could not bear
The thought this might her fluffy tail impair.
So she decided that she'd wait a bit instead.
Were not the village folk all still in bed?
Perhaps the ice would melt as morning warmed.
Then she could get her tail away unharmed.
And so she waited by the lake
Until she heard the village wake
And knew that she could wait no longer.
She pulled and tugged – the ice had gotten stronger;
It held on tight to her poor tail.
She thrashed and writhed to no avail.
But luckily her friend the Wolf came by.
"Dear Wolf, my cousin!" came her cry,
"Please help me, for my tail's stuck fast.
If you can't save me I'll soon breathe my last."
And like a friend the Wolf came to her aid.
And short work of her problem quickly made,
By biting off her tail to set her free.
The tailless Fox limped homeward gratefully.
For though she'd lost her tail, the Wolf had saved her skin.

It's not obscure the moral found herein:
If you would keep your tail, well, then you must prepare,
When things start getting tough, to sacrifice some hair.

Свинья под Дубом

Свинья под Дубом вековым
Наелась желудей досыта, до отвала;
Наевшись, выспалась под ним;
Потом, глаза продравши, встала
И рылом подрывать у Дуба корни стала.
“Ведь это дереву вредит, –
Ей с Дубу Ворон говорит, –
Коль корни обнажишь, оно засохнуть может”.
“Пусть сохнет, – говорит Свинья, –
Ничуть меня то не тревожит,
В нём проку мало вижу я;
Хоть век его не будь, ничуть не пожалею;
Лишь были б жёлуди: ведь я от них жирею”. –
“Неблагодарная! – примолвил Дуб ей тут, –
Когда бы вверх могла поднять ты рыло,
Тебе бы видно было,
Что эти жёлуди на мне растут”.

Невежда так же в ослепленье
Бранит науку и ученье
И все учёные труды,
Не чувствуя, что он вкушает их плоды.

The Sow Beneath the Oak

A Sow, most fond of acorns, found enough
One day to eat her fill. She was so stuffed
She went to sleep right there, and when she woke
Began to root around beneath an Oak.
"Stop that at once, the forest's not your sty,"
A Raven cried out angrily.
"If you expose its roots this Oak will die."
Said Sow, "So let it die, what's that to me?
I would not care if there were none left in this wood.
It's acorns that I care for – boy, do they taste good!"
"Ungrateful Sow," the Oak then said,
"If only you could raise your head
And look aloft you'd see
That all the acorns you so love – they grow on me!"

Those fools who curse all science and its fruits
Are like a Sow who digs up oak tree roots –
Too blind to see the science they abuse
Gives rise to many things that they delight to use.

Лягушки, просящие Царя

Лягушкам стало не угодно
Правление народно,
И показалось им совсем не благородно
Без службы и на воле жить.
Чтоб горю пособить,
То стали у богов Царя они просить.
Хоть слушать всякий вздор богам бы и не сродно,
На сей, однакож, раз послушал их Зевес:
Дал им Царя. Летит к ним с шумом Царь с небес,
И плотно так он треснулся на царство,
Что ходенем пошло трясинно государство:
Со всех Лягушки ног
В испуге пометались,
Кто как успел, куда кто мог,
И шёпотом Царю по кельям дивовались.
И подлинно, что Царь на диво был им дан:
Не суетлив, не вертопрашен,
Степенен, молчалив и важен;
Дородством, ростом великан,
Ну, посмотреть, так это чудо!
Одно в Царе лишь было худо:
Царь этот был осиновый чурбан.
Сначала, чтя его особу превысоку,
Не смеет подступить из подданных никто:
Со страхом на него глядят они, и то
Украдкой, издали, сквозь аир и осоку;
Но так как в свете чуда нет,
К которому б не пригляделся свет,
То и они сперва от страху отдохнули,
Потом к Царю подползть с преданностью дерзнули;
Сперва перед Царём ничком;
А тем, кто посмелей, дай сесть к нему бочком:
Дай попытаться сесть с ним рядом;
А тем, которые ещё поудалей,
К царю садятся уж и задом.
Царь терпит всё по милости своей.
Немного погодя, посмотришь, кто захочет,
Тот на него и вскочит.
В три дня наскучило с таким Царем житьё.
Лягушки новое челобитьё,

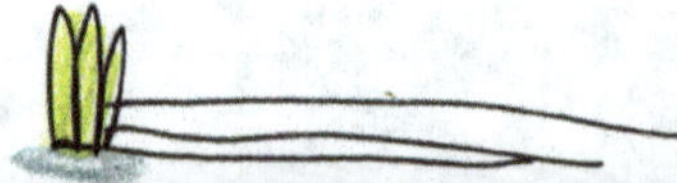

The Frogs Who Begged for a Tsar

Some Frogs who'd lived without a monarch for a while
Had heard self-government was out of style;
They thought democracy passé, I guess,
Or that it lacked a certain, well, noblesse.
They wondered where to find a Tsar fit for their use
And thought it best to ask for one from Zeus,
Who normally ignores such foolish prayers,
But somehow felt the urge to answer theirs.
He tossed one down from his high mountain top.
Into the swamp it fell and made a mighty plop,
And shook the earth with such a crashing sound
That Frogs went dashing all around
And hid themselves in fright.
They marveled at this Tsar that Zeus had sent,
One worthy of their awe and wonderment –
Enormous, solemn, calm – a most imposing sight,
His manner regal and imperious,
Composed and silent – serious.
He'd but one fault to balance all this good:
This Tsar was just a block of wood.
At first his subjects, paralyzed by awe and fear,
Quite lacked the daring to approach too near
And only peeked at their new Tsar
Between their fingers from afar.
But everywhere, throughout eternity,
There's never been a sight so terrible or strange
That people will not crowd around to see.
And frogs are just the same. So things began to change.
At first the Frogs approached kowtowing.
And then, emboldened, started merely bowing.
And since the Tsar did nothing to object,
They showed increasing disrespect.
Before too long the Frogs were swarming over him,
As if he were some froggy jungle gym.
But soon they found this silent Tsar a bore

Чтоб им Юпитер в их болотную державу
Дал подлинно Царя на славу!
Молитвам тёплым их внемля,
Послал Юпитер к ним на царство Журавля.
Царь этот не чурбан, совсем иного нраву:
Не любит баловать народа своего;
Он виноватых ест: а на суде его
Нет правых никого;
Зато уж у него,
Что завтрак, что обед, что ужин, то расправа.
На жителей болот
Приходит чёрный год.
В Лягушках каждый день великий недочёт.
С утра до вечера их Царь по царству ходит
И всякого, кого ни встретит он,
Тотчас засудит и – проглотит.
Вот пуще прежнего и кваканье и стон,
Чтоб им Юпитер снова
Пожаловал Царя инова;
Что нынешний их Царь глотает их, как мух;
Что даже им нельзя (как это ни ужасно!)
Ни носа выставить, ни квакнуть безопасно;
Что, наконец, их Царь тошнее им засух.
"Почто ж вы прежде жить счастливо не умели?
Не мне ль, безумные, – вещал им с неба глас, –
Покоя не было от вас?
Не вы ли о Царе мне уши прошумели?
Вам дан был Царь? – так тот был слишком тих:
Вы взбунтовались в вашей луже,
Другой вам дан – так этот слишком лих:
Живите с ним, чтоб не было вам хуже!"

And so petitioned mighty Zeus once more.
Now asking that Tsar Woodblock be replaced
With one who'd bring more glory to their race.
Great Zeus complied and sent them down a Crane,
A Tsar unlike the wood one; that was plain.
While Woodblock showed benevolence,
Tsar Crane devoured all who gave offense.
And in his court it soon appeared,
No matter what the crime, no Frog was ever cleared.
Each Frog he saw, the Tsar would sentence to be swallowed.
So he consumed his subjects morning, noon and night.
They suffered through the awful year that followed.
At last they prayed to Zeus to help them in their plight,
"He's eating us like flies, we cannot venture out
Or even croak out loud.
Soon frogs will be extinct, without a doubt."
They called this Tsar's behavior a disgrace,
And asked Great Zeus to send a new one in his place.
Then Zeus's voice boomed down; at last he'd had enough
Of these fool Frogs. He sternly gave them this rebuff:
"Why were you not content with what you had?
You lived in peace; your lives were not half bad.
I sent the Woodblock Tsar to silence your complaints.
And as a Tsar, I'd say, he ranked among the saints.
But no, you found him much too silent, mild, serene;
And now you dare to say the second one's too mean.
I'll warn you only once: best keep the Tsar you curse;
The next one that I send you might be worse."

Кот и Повар

Какой-то Повар, грамотей,
С поварни побежал своей
В кабак (он набожных был правил
И в этот день по куме тризну правил),
А дома стеречи съестное от мышей
Кота оставил.
Но что же, возвратясь, он видит? На полу
Объедки пирога; а Васька – Кот в углу,
Припав за уксусным бочонком,
Мурлыча и ворча, трудится над курчонком.
"Ах ты, обжора! ах, злодей! –
Тут Ваську Повар укоряет, –
Не стыдно ль стен тебе, не только что людей?
(А Васька всё-таки курчонка убирает.)
Как! быв честным Котом до этих пор,
Бывало, за пример тебя смиренства кажут, –
А ты... ахти какой позор!
Теперя все соседи скажут:
"Кот Васька плут! Кот Васька вор!
И Ваську-де не только что в поварню,
Пускать не надо и на двор,
Как волка жадного в овчарню:
Он порча, он чума, он язва здешних мест!"
(А Васька слушает, да ест.)
Тут ритор мой, дав волю слов теченью,
Не находил конца нравоученью.
Но что ж? Пока его он пел,
Кот Васька всё жаркое съел.

А я бы повару иному
Велел на стенке зарубить:
Чтоб там речей не тратить попустому,
Где нужно власть употребить.

The Cat and the Cook

A Cook, before his daily work was ended,
For sake of sacred duty, left his post untended.
You see his friend had died and 'twas his obligation
To honor him by drinking a libation.
To keep away the mice who might intrude,
He left his Cat (called Vaska) there to guard the food.
When from the tavern he returned in spirits gay,
Upon the kitchen floor he saw, to his dismay,
A mostly eaten pie, while his assistant, Cat,
Had hidden in the corner and started on a fat
Roast chicken that had been left out to cool.
"Oh you glutton, oh you knave, oh you sneaky fool,"
The Cook reproached his Cat. "I can't believe my eyes.
I thought you could be trusted not to steal my pies.
Oh, shame on you, my Vaska. Oh, for shame.
You've brought dishonor to your name.
And all around the neighborhood,
The folks who used to think you good
And give you kitchen scraps and stuff
Will turn against you soon enough.
No one will feed you anymore,
They'll chase you from their kitchen door.
Because of all the food you took,
They'll call you scum and thief and crook."
Now Vaska meekly listened, as befits a sinner,
Repentantly he sighed, but kept on eating dinner.
As on and on the Cook's fine sermon droned,
Sly Vaska stripped the roast down to the bone.

What kind of fool would moralize
And watch a thief enjoying loot before his eyes?
No one who steals will e'er repent of it
When he's allowed to reap the benefit.
If you would cause a thief to change,
Well then, you really must arrange
Not only that he be admonished,
But also duly punished.

Лев на ловле

Собака, Лев да Волк с Лисой
В соседстве как-то жили,
И вот какой
Между собой
Они завет все положили:
Чтоб им зверей съобща ловить,
И что наловится, всё поровну делить.
Не знаю, как и чем, а знаю, что сначала
Лиса оленя поймала
И шлёт к товарищам послов,
Чтоб шли делить счастливый лов:
Добыча, право, недурная!
Пришли, пришёл и Лев; он, когти разминая
И озираючи товарищей кругом,
Делёж располагает
И говорит: "Мы, братцы, вчетвером. –
И начетверо он оленя раздирает. –
Теперь давай делить! Смотрите же, друзья;
Вот эта часть моя
По договору;
Вот эта мне, как Льву, принадлежит без спору;
Вот эта мне за то, что всех сильнее я;
А к этой чуть из вас лишь лапу кто протянет,
Тот с места жив не встанет".

The Lion on a Hunt

A Dog, a Fox, a Lion and a Wolf, all neighbors,
Had made a plan that they'd combine their labors
When each went hunting prey.
And all declared that they
Would share alike what each one caught,
As hunting partners surely ought.
The Fox became the first one to succeed.
She caught a deer who'd stopped too long to feed.
Delighted with this prize,
The Fox sent out a message to apprise
Her friends of it and tell them to come share.
The hungry Lion saw the rest already there
And volunteered to divvy up the deer.
He said: "Let's see, my partners, there are four of us."
He cut it into fourths and was most scrupulous
To make them like in size. "The first piece," he decreed,
"Is mine, as we agreed.
The second is my due as King, I think that's clear.
The third's mine too for being strongest here.
As for the fourth, if any wants to make it
Away from here alive, he will not take it."

Ворона и Лисица

Уж сколько раз твердили миру,
Что лесть гнусна, вредна; но только всё не впрок,
И в сердце льстец всегда отыщет уголок.

Вороне где-то бог послал кусочек сыру;
На ель Ворона взгромоздясь,
Позавтракать было совсем уж собралась,
Да позадумалась, а сыр во рту держала.
На ту беду Лиса близёхонько бежала;
Вдруг сырный дух Лису остановил:
Лисица видит сыр, Лисицу сыр пленил,
Плутовка к дереву на цыпочках подходит;
Вертит хвостом, с Вороны глаз не сводит
И говорит так сладко, чуть дыша:
"Голубушка, как хороша!
Ну что за шейка, что за глазки!
Рассказывать, так, право, сказки!
Какие перушки! какой носок!
И, верно, ангельский быть должен голосок!
Спой, светик, не стыдись!
Что ежели, сестрица, Одна строчка
При красоте такой и петь ты мастерица, –
Ведь ты б у нас была царь-птица!"
Вещуньина с похвал вскружилась голова,
От радости в зобу дыханье спёрло, –
И на приветливы Лисицыны слова
Ворона каркнула во всё воронье горло:
Сыр выпал – с ним была плутовка такова.

The Crow and the Fox

It's often said, and each of us agrees,
That flattery does harm and is a scoundrel's art.
Yet somehow flattering words find ways to reach each heart.

One lucky day Miss Crow got hold of cheese,
And flying up with it into the nearest tree,
She sat and clutched it in her beak for all to see,
And savored this fine tasty meal she'd found.
Alas, just then a Fox passed by upon the ground
And sniffed a cheesy smell from up above.
He spied the cheese; and then Fox fell in love.
Up to that tree the sly one crept on tippy toe;
He twirled his tail and kept his eyes upon Miss Crow,
And in a voice so sweet it made you sick he said:
"What lovely bird sits here above my head?
Such sparkling eyes, such shiny feathers too,
She looks just like a fairy tale come true.
What tail, what talons, what a beak!
What voice she must have when she's moved to speak,
Or better yet to sing! Please let me hear your voice!
If you can sing the way you look, we'll all rejoice;
For we'll have found our queen, you'll be our choice!"
Though wise, Miss Crow could not resist such praise;
Her mind was in a whirl, her breath caught in her crop;
The Fox's honeyed words had gone right to her head.
She croaked with open throat and let the morsel drop.
The sly Fox snatched it up and off with it he sped.

Квартет

Проказница-Мартышка,
  Осёл,
  Козёл
Да косолапый Мишка
Затеяли сыграть Квартет.
Достали нот, баса, альта, две скрипки
И сели на лужок под липки, –
Пленять своим искусством свет.
Ударили в смычки, дерут, а толку нет.
"Стой, братцы, стой! – кричит Мартышка. – Погодите!
Как музыке идти? Ведь вы не так сидите.
Ты с басом, Мишенька, садись против альта,
Я, прима, сяду против вторы;
Тогда пойдёт уж музыка не та:
У нас запляшут лес и горы!"
Расселись, начали Квартет;
Он всё-таки на лад нейдёт.
"Постойте ж, я сыскал секрет, –
Кричит Осёл, – мы, верно, уж поладим,
Коль рядом сядем".
Послушались Осла: уселись чинно в ряд,
А всё-таки Квартет нейдёт на лад.
Вот пуще прежнего пошли у них разборы
И споры,
Кому и как сидеть.
Случилось Соловью на шум их прилететь.
Тут с просьбой все к нему, чтоб их решить сомненье:
"Пожалуй, – говорят, – возьми на час терпенье,
Чтобы Квартет в порядок наш привесть:
И ноты есть у нас, и инструменты есть;
Скажи лишь, как нам сесть!" –
"Чтоб музыкантом быть, так надобно уменье
И уши ваших понежней, –
Им отвечает Соловей, –
А вы, друзья, как ни садитесь,
Всё в музыканты не годитесь".

The String Quartet

A brown, bow-legged Bear,
  A Monkey,
  A Donkey,
And Billy Goat, on a dare,
Agreed they'd form a string quartet.
They got hold of a score, four kinds of fiddle,
Then they sat down with Monkey in the middle
And thought, "It's easy, we're all set!"
Put bow to string: alas, no music could they get!
Then Monkey shouted: "Stop, we have not got the sound!
How can we do this right, we're sitting wrong way round!
Come, Goat, sit there, that's a good fellow.
Our playing now's sure to entrance.
And Bear you're here, pray, bring your cello.
The forests, hills and fields will dance!"
So changing places they began their playing
But still it sounded worse than Donkey's braying.
Then, "Stop, I've got it now, heed what I'm saying!"
Cried Goat, "If we sit thus, our music cannot flow.
The secret is we must sit in a row."
And sitting in a row, as they'd been told,
They made a racket that would make your blood run cold.
No music that they played could they get right!
So they began to argue and to fight
About how best to sit. They got so loud
That Nightingale flew down to check things out.
And seeing that great maestro, in a trice,
The four began to ask him for advice.
"Oh, maestro, tell us how to make our music sweet.
Our instruments are new; our score's complete.
So all we need to know is where to put each seat."
The music expert answered, "To make music that is nice,
You have to practice hard to train your hand and ear.
To learn this craft takes better gifts than yours, I fear.
To make fine music there's no way that you'll be fit,
My friends, no matter how you sit."

Зеркало и Обезьяна

Мартышка, в Зеркале увидя образ свой,
Тихохонько Медведя толк ногой:
"Смотри-ка, – говорит, – кум милый мой!
Что это там за рожа?
Какие у неё ужимки и прыжки!
Я удавилась бы с тоски,
Когда бы на неё хоть чуть была похожа.
А ведь, признайся, есть
Из кумушек моих таких кривляк пять – шесть:
Я даже их могу по пальцам перечесть". –
"Чем кумушек считать трудиться,
Не лучше ль на себя, кума, оборотиться?" –
Ей Мишка отвечал.
Но Мишенькин совет лишь попусту пропал.

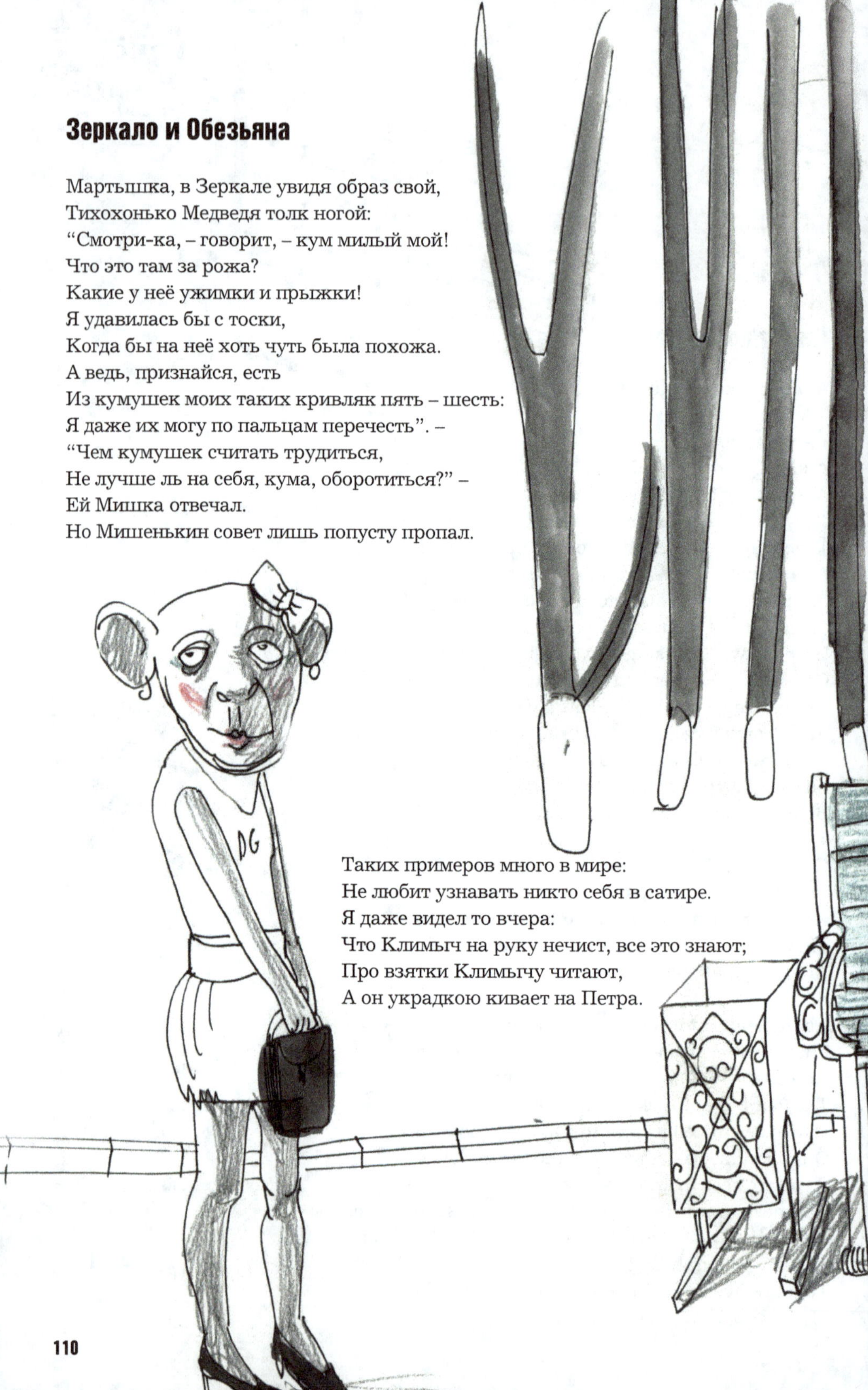

Таких примеров много в мире:
Не любит узнавать никто себя в сатире.
Я даже видел то вчера:
Что Климыч на руку нечист, все это знают;
Про взятки Климычу читают,
А он украдкою кивает на Петра.

The Looking Glass and the Monkey

Once Monkey saw her image in a glass,
And poked her friend, a Bear, who'd chanced to pass,
"Come here and see this simpering lass!
Her mug is ugly past belief,
And yet she's so affected.
I myself would die of grief
If that were me reflected.
And yet you know, it seems to me
Some likeness to my friends are there for all to see.
I must know five or six who smirk unnaturally."
"Now, counting flaws in friends won't get you anywhere!
Best think about what makes your own self less than fair,"
Was Bear's advice, much needed,
But like good folk around the world, the Monkey failed to heed it.

Now satire too's a looking glass,
In which we fail to see ourselves, alas.
To what's portrayed we close our eyes,
Though all the world can recognize
Whose faults are being satirized.

Мартышка и Очки

Мартышка к старости слаба глазами стала;
А у людей она слыхала,
Что это зло ещё не так большой руки:
Лишь стоит завести Очки.
Очков с полдюжины себе она достала;
Вертит Очками так и сяк:
То к темю их прижмёт, то их на хвост нанижет,
То их понюхает, то их полижет;
Очки не действуют никак.
"Тьфу пропасть! – говорит она, – и тот дурак,
Кто слушает людских всех врак:
Всё про Очки лишь мне налгали;
А проку на – волос нет в них".
Мартышка тут с досады и с печали
О камень так хватила их,
Что только брызги засверкали.

К несчастью, то ж бывает у людей:
Как ни полезна вещь, – цены не зная ей,
Невежда про неё свой толк всё к худу клонит;
А ежели невежда познатней,
Так он её ещё и гонит.

The Monkey and the Spectacles

Miss Monkey's eyes began to fail as she got old,
But she did not despair, for she'd been told
That humans had a cure for this disease,
And spectacles would help her see with ease.
She went right out and bought five or six pair,
And snatched them up and stuck them here and there.
She put them round her neck and on her tail.
Then sniffed and licked them, but to no avail,
For nothing that she did improved her eyes.
She thought, "It serves me right for listening to such lies.
All beasts who trust men's words deserve the booby prize.
These spectacles are nothing but a waste of cash,
They are no use – I should have known."
She grabbed her specs quick as a flash
And threw them down upon a stone.
And into pieces they all smashed.

The world of men knows of such cases too,
When fools ignore the worth of something new.
For, since they cannot understand it,
They call it names and say it will not do,
While those who have the power try to ban it.

Собачья дружба

У кухни под окном
На солнышке Полкан с Барбосом, лёжа, грелись.
Хоть у ворот перед двором
Пристойнее б стеречь им было дом,
Но как они уж понаелись –
И вежливые ж псы притом
Ни на кого не лают днём –
Так рассуждать они пустилися вдвоём
О всякой всячине: о их собачьей службе,
О худе, о добре и, наконец, о дружбе.
“Что может, – говорит Полкан, – приятней быть,
Как с другом сердце к сердцу жить;
Во всём оказывать взаимную услугу;
Не спить без друга и не съесть,
Стоять горой за дружню шерсть ,
И, наконец, в глаза глядеть друг другу,
Чтоб только улучить счастливый час,
Нельзя ли друга чем потешить, позабавить,
И в дружнем счастье всё своё блаженство ставить!
Вот если б, например, с тобой у нас
Такая дружба завелась:
Скажу я смело,
Мы б и не видели, как время бы летело”. –
“А что же? Это дело! –
Барбос ответствует ему: –
Давно, Полканушка, мне больно самому,

Friendship Among Dogs

Once in the kitchen yard,
Two dogs, named Prince and Duke, lay dozing in the sun.
They really should have been out front on guard,
But, having eaten well and hard,
They felt their workday must be done.
Thus, side-by-side they lay,
Much too polite to bark by day,
And got to chatting in a doggy way:
Discussing doggy lives and sharing doggy dreams.
And then talk turned to friendship, so it seems.
Said Prince, "What pleasure can compare
With having a true friend with whom to share
Each cat we chase and every snooze we snooze;
To fight against intruders, win or lose;
To bark and bay together in a chorus;
And split the table scraps the cook saves for us;
To gaze into our friend's brown doggy eyes;
And think no other pooch is half so brave and wise.
If you and I were friends like this, I dare to say,
We'd find our lives improved in an important way.
Come on, let's try – we'll start this very day!"
The other dog replied,
"It's pained me, I confide,

Что, бывши одного двора с тобой собаки,
Мы дня не проживём без драки;
И из чего? Спасибо господам:
Ни голодно, ни тесно нам!
Притом же, право, стыдно:
Пёс дружества слывёт примером с давних дней.
А дружбы между псов, как будто меж людей,
Почти совсем не видно". –
"Явим же в ней пример мы в наши времена! –
Вскричал Полкан, – дай лапу!" – "Вот она!"
И новые друзья ну обниматься,
Ну целоваться;
Не знают с радости, к кому и приравняться:
"Орест мой!" – "Мой Пилад!"
Прочь свары, зависть, злость!
Тут повар на беду из кухни кинул кость.
Вот новые друзья к ней взапуски несутся:
Где делся и совет и лад?
С Пиладом мой Орест грызутся, –
Лишь только клочья вверх летят:
Насилу наконец их розлили водою.

Свет полон дружбою такою.
Про нынешних друзей льзя молвить, не греша.
Что в дружбе все они едва ль не одинаки:
Послушать – кажется, одна у них душа, –
А только кинь им кость, так что твои собаки

That, though we share the same yard day and night,
No single day can pass without a fight.
We do not have to fight in order to survive
Our master's rich enough for both of us to thrive.
And I must say that I am full of shame
That, though the friendship dogs show man is famous everywhere,
True friendship dog-to-dog is really rather rare.
And for this shameful fact, we've only dogs to blame.
Let's both work hard to aid this cause."
Cried Prince, "Let's shake!" and they clasped paws,
And hugged. all tender-hearted
And vowed not to be parted.
When they had called each other every name they could employ
Like "brother mine" and "my true pal" and even "buddy boy,"
The cook tossed them a bone right from his pot,
And all their plans for friendship they forgot.
For falling on that bone as if they'd never see another,
Regardless of the love that they'd just vowed,
They snarled and bit the dog they'd just called "brother,"
And fur flew up around them in a cloud.

In human life such friendships are not rare.
Some friends profess such love you'd think they'd always share,
But let there be some prize that each wants for his own,
They'll start to fight like two dogs with one bone.

Крестьянин и Змея

Змея к Крестьянину пришла проситься в дом,
Не по – пустому жить без дела,
Нет, нянчить у него детей она хотела:
Хлеб слаще нажитый трудом!
“Я знаю, – говорит она, – худую славу,
Которая у вас, людей,
Идёт про Змей,
Что все они презлого нраву;
Из древности гласит молва,
Что благодарности они не знают,
Что нет у них ни дружбы, ни родства.
Что даже собственных детей они съедают.
Всё это может быть: но я не такова.
Я сроду никого не только не кусала,
Но так гнушаюсь зла,
Что жало у себя я вырвать бы дала,
Когда б я знала,
Что жить могу без жала;
И, словом, я добрей
Всех Змей.
Суди ж, как буду я любить твоих детей!” –
“Коль это, – говорит Крестьянин, – и не ложно,
Все мне принять тебя не можно;
Когда пример такой
У нас полюбят,
Тогда вползут сюда за доброю Змеёй,
Одной,
Сто злых и всех детей здесь перегубят.
Да, кажется, голубушка моя,
И потому с тобой мне не ужиться,
Что лучшая Змея,
По мне ни к чёрту не годится”.

Отцы, понятно ль вам, на что здесь мечу я?..

The Peasant and the Snake

A Snake applied for work as child's nursemaid
Within a Peasant house where one was sought.
"I can't bear idleness," she said.
"I want to be of use instead.
I know, of course, that most men are afraid
Of snakes, for men have all been taught,
Since ancient times, how evil snakes can be:
Without capacity to love or feel –
They'll eat their young before they skip a meal.
That may be true of some, but not of me,
For I have never bitten anyone.
I'd gladly tear my fangs out, if it could be done.
And all my life I have done only good.
If only you would hire me, I would
Just dote upon your children. Put me to the test.
You'll see I am a snake unlike the rest."
The Peasant gave her this reply,
"Well, even if that's true and not a lie,
Still never will I hire you, Miss Snake.
For there's a risk I cannot take:
That once the word got out
That snakes are welcome here, without a doubt,
You will be followed by your brothers,
Not the good ones, but the others!
And soon our boys and girls would start to die.
But there's another reason why:
The best of all the Snakes who've walked the earth
Have never seemed to me of any worth."

You heads of households, for your children's sakes,
Recall this fable when you deal with snakes.

Прохожие и Собаки

Шли два приятеля вечернею порой
И дельный разговор вели между собой,
Как вдруг из подворотни
Дворняжка тявкнула на них;
За ней другая, там ещё две-три, и вмиг
Со всех дворов Собак сбежалося с полсотни.
Один было уже Прохожий камень взял.
"И, полно, братец!" – тут другой ему сказал, –
Собак ты не уймёшь от лаю,
Лишь пуще всю раздразнишь стаю;
Пойдём вперёд: я их натуру лучше знаю".
И подлинно, прошли шагов десятков пять,
Собаки начали помалу затихать,
И стало, наконец, совсем их не слыхать.

Завистники, на что ни взглянут,
Подымут вечно лай;
А ты себе своей дорогою ступай:
Полают, да отстанут.

The Passersby and the Dogs

One evening, two good friends, in search of relaxation,
Were strolling slowly, deep in conversation,
When all at once, from nowhere, came a mongrel yowling.
From everywhere ran more and more,
Until they formed a canine corps –
All barking, yelping, growling.
One friend picked up a nearby stone
And made to throw it.
The other said, "Leave them alone,
They'll just bark more if that is thrown.
If we walk by, they'll quiet down before you know it.
I know dogs well: they soon grow bored
When they're ignored."
And so the friends strolled calmly down the hill.
The noise died down at once and very soon was still.

The envious, when you attract their eye,
Will bark at you like any mongrel pup.
But if you pass serenely by,
They'll yelp a bit and then shut up.

Цветы

В отворённом окне богатого покоя,
В фарфоровых расписанных горшках,
Цветы поддельные, с живыми вместе стоя,
На проволочных стебельках
Качалися спесиво
И выставляли всем красу свою на диво.
Вот дождик начал накрапать.
Цветы тафтяные Юпитера тут просят:
Нельзя ли дождь унять;
Дождь всячески они ругают и поносят.
"Юпитер! – молятся, – ты дождик прекрати,
Что в нём пути
И что его на свете хуже?
Смотри, нельзя по улице пройти:
Везде лишь от него и грязь, и лужи".
Однако же Зевес не внял мольбе пустой,
И дождь себе прошёл своею полосой.
Прогнавши зной,
Он воздух прохладил; природа оживилась,
И зелень вся как будто обновилась.
Тогда и на окне Цветы живые все
Раскинулись во всей своей красе
И стали от дождя душистей,
Свежее и пушистей.
А бедные Цветы поддельные с тех пор
Лишились всей красы и брошены на двор,
Как сор.

Таланты истинны за критику не злятся:
Их повредить она не может красоты;
Одни поддельные цветы
Дождя боятся.

The Flowers

Within a richly furnished room, there stood
Some pots of flowers – silk and fresh together –
Right near an open window where they could
Enjoy the summer weather.
Alas, fresh flowers wilt in too much heat,
But not the silk ones, fueling their conceit.
They twisted haughtily on stems of wire,
Inviting all the world to come admire.
Just then the rain began to fall.
The silken flowers liked this not at all.
They prayed to Zeus to make it go away.
They said that rain destroys a summer day
And leads to puddles, mud and disarray.
But Zeus such foolish talk ignored.
Down from the sky the water poured,
And nature flourished everywhere
From rainfall's cooling of the air.
Among the flowers in the room,
The real ones were restored,
Upright and full and fragrant as before,
When in full bloom.
The silk ones fared much worse, without a doubt.
Their beauty was no more;
Their owner threw them out.

No critic can destroy a talent that is real –
Its beauty can't be stained.
And only artificial flowers feel
Afraid of rain.

Ворона

Когда не хочешь быть смешон,
Держися звания, в котором ты рождён.
Простолюдин со знатью не роднися;
И если карлой сотворён,
То в великаны не тянися,
А помни свой ты чаще рост.

Утыкавши себе павлиньим перьем хвост,
Ворона с Павами пошла гулять спесиво –
И думает, что на неё
Родня и прежние приятели её
Все заглядятся, как на диво;
Что Павам всем она сестра
И что пришла её пора
Быть украшением Юнонина двора.
Какой же вышел плод её высокомерья?
Что Павами она ощипана кругом,
И что, бежав от них, едва не кувырком,
Не говоря уж о чужом,
На ней и своего осталось мало перья.
Она было назад к своим; но те совсем
Заклёванной Вороны не узнали,
Ворону вдосталь ощипали,
И кончились её затеи тем,
Что от Ворон она отстала,
А к Павам не пристала.

Я эту басенку вам былью поясню.
Матрёне, дочери купецкой, мысль припала,
Чтоб в знатную войти родню.
Приданого за ней полмиллиона.
Вот выдали Матрёну за барона.
Что ж вышло? Новая родня ей колет глаз
Попрёком, что она мещанкой родилась,
А старая за то, что к знатным приплелась:
И сделалась моя Матрёна
Ни Пава, ни Ворона.

The Crow

If you don't want to be the butt of mirth,
Don't try to rise above your birth.
The peasant and the noble can't be kin.
We all thrive best where we by birth fit in.

A Crow once stuck some peacock feathers in her tail.
She thought she'd be the envy of her friends and kin
And that the Peacock clan would take her in.
But Fate decrees that all such plans will fail.
And when they saw the Crow in Peacock clothes,
The Peacocks' fury rose:
They rushed in to attack,
And with their beaks they got their feathers back
And plucked out most of Crow's.
At last she could escape;
She fled back home in awful shape –
A sadder, balder bird, but wiser.
Alas, her kinfolk failed to recognize her
Without her coat of shining black.
They too attacked and drove her back.
The end result of all her social climbing plans
Was exile from them both – the Crow and Peacock clans.

The first tale was a fable, but the next is true:
The daughter of a merchant, very well to do,
Decided she would marry into high estate.
Her dowry was so large, that wasn't hard to do –
Soon she had a baron for her mate.
And the result? No one will be surprised:
By all she was despised.
By her new husband's folk, because they thought her low.
And by her own, because they felt she thought them so.
And so the bride was fully ostracized,
For though she was no Peacock, nor was she a Crow.

Трудолюбивый Медведь

Увидя, что мужик, трудяся над дугами,
Их прибыльно сбывает с рук
(А дуги гнут с терпеньем и не вдруг),
Медведь задумал жить такими же трудами.
Пошёл по лесу треск и стук,
И слышно за версту проказу.
Орешника, березника и вязу
Мой Мишка погубил несметное число,
А не даётся ремесло.
Вот идёт к мужику он попросить совета
И говорит: “Сосед, что за причина эта?
Деревья – таки я ломать могу,
А не согнул ни одного в дугу.
Скажи, в чём есть тут главное уменье?” –
“В том, – отвечал сосед, – Чего в тебе, кум, вовсе нет:
В терпенье”.

The Hardworking Bear

A Bear once watched a peasant making harness yokes
By bending into bows thin trunks of trees,
And selling them for cash to neighbor folks.
But what he failed to see, this Bear,
Was that producing bow shaped yokes like these
Requires patience, time and care.
The Bear decided he'd take up this trade
And, despite the awful noise he made,
The trees he tried to bend just snapped in two.
So after he'd destroyed more than a few,
He went to ask the peasant what to do.
"Good Sir," said he, "I bend the trees so hard they break,
But cannot make them take the proper shape.
Yet every one you touch becomes a perfect bow.
Pray tell me what your secret is, I'd really love to know."
"Friend Bear, it isn't that I have some special skill or knack;
But merely that I've patience, which you lack."

Волк и Волчёнок

Волчёнка Волк, начав помалу приучать
Отцовским промыслом питаться,
Послал его опушкой прогуляться;
А между тем велел прилежней примечать,
Нельзя ль где счастья им отведать:
Хоть, захватя греха,
На счёт бы пастуха
Позавтракать иль пообедать!
Приходит ученик домой
И говорит: "Пойдём скорей со мной!
Обед готов; ничто не может быть вернее:
Там под горой
Пасут овец, одна другой жирнее;
Любую стоит лишь унесть
И съесть;
А стадо таково, что трудно перечесть". –
"Постой-ка, – Волк сказал, – сперва мне ведать надо,
Каков пастух у стада?" –
"Хоть говорят, что он
Не плох, заботлив и умён,
Однако стадо я обшёл со всех сторон
И высмотрел собак: они совсем не жирны,
И плохи, кажется, и смирны. –
"Меня так этот слух, –
Волк старый говорит, – не очень к стаду манит;
Коль подлинно не плох пастух,
Так он плохих собак держать не станет.
Тут тотчас попадёшь в беду!
Пойдём-ка, я тебя на стадо наведу,
Где сбережём верней мы наши шкуры:
Хотя при стаде том и множество собак,
Да сам пастух дурак;
А где пастух дурак, там и собаки дуры".

The Wolf and His Cub

A Wolf Cub's training had begun
In all the skills he'd need when he was grown.
One day Wolf Father asked his son
To strike out fully on his own,
Beyond the woods, and try to scout
Among the flocks at pasture thereabout,
To find ones where the shepherd had grown lax,
Providing easy prey for small wolf packs
To help themselves to meals and extra snacks.
The Cub returned, quite proud and pleased,
And said, "I've found a flock just asking to be seized.
Our supper's grazing on a nearby slope,
As fat as any wolf could hope,
So many that we all can pick and choose.
Come on, come on, there is no time to lose."
Wolf Father said, "Now son, just wait a bit,
The flock sounds good, but who's in charge of it?"
"They say the shepherd's not half bad –
A smart, hard-working lad.
But yet the dogs seem lazy, meek and small.
I do not think that they are on the ball,
And likely won't put up much fight at all."
The older Wolf just shook his head
At this report and said,
"For us this flock holds little hope,
For if the shepherd is no dope,
He won't choose dogs that shirk.
And good dogs keep us from our work.
Come on, my son, I'll take you to
A flock as safe as any,
For though the dogs on guard are many,
The shepherd is a fool. And when that's true,
It follows that the dogs are foolish too."

Ларчик

Случается нередко нам
И труд и мудрость видеть там,
Где стоит только догадаться
За дело просто взяться.

К кому-то принесли от мастера Ларец.
Отделкой, чистотой Ларец в глаза кидался;
Ну, всякий Ларчиком прекрасным любовался.
Вот входит в комнату механики мудрец.
Взглянув на Ларчик, он сказал: "Ларец с секретом,
Так; он и без замка;
А я берусь открыть; да, да, уверен в этом;
Не смейтесь так исподтишка!
Я отыщу секрет и Ларчик вам открою:
В механике и я чего-нибудь да стою".
Вот за Ларец принялся он:
Вертит его со всех сторон
И голову свою ломает;
То гвоздик, то другой, то скобку пожимает.
Тут, глядя на него, иной
Качает головой;
Те шепчутся, а те смеются меж собой.
В ушах лишь только отдаётся:
"Не тут, не так, не там!" Механик пуще рвётся.
Потел, потел; но наконец устал,
От Ларчика отстал
И, как открыть его, никак не догадался;
А Ларчик просто открывался.

The Treasure Chest

At times we think that it takes toil and complex thought
To solve some problem, when we ought
To take a simple and straightforward route,
For often it is this that bears best fruit.

A craftsman brought his countrymen great pleasure
By making wooden chests for holding treasure.
A man received a gift of one of these.
What carpentry, what carving – what a masterpiece!
His friends all came to see the chest he had received,
Including one "mechanic" who believed
He knew how every single thing was made
And all the secret tricks of every trade.
He said, "This is no simple wooden box,
It does not open with a key,
Just look, it has no locks;
But no such box can baffle me.
Just give it here.
I'll learn its secrets, never fear."
He did work hard, he really tried:
He turned the chest from side to side,
And pressed and tapped it all around,
But still remained quite mystified,
And long before the trick was found,
Exhausted, he conceded.
And so returned the chest, defeated.
How did it open? Have you guessed?
You simply raise its lid, like any other chest.

Муравей

Какой-то Муравей был силы непомерной,
Какой не слыхано ни в древни времена;
Он даже (говорит его историк верной)
Мог поднимать больших ячменных два зерна!
Притом и в храбрости за чудо почитался:
Где б ни завидел червяка,
Тотчас в него впивался
И даже хаживал один на паука.
А тем вошёл в такую славу
Он в муравейнике своём,
Что только и речей там было, что о нём.
Я лишние хвалы считаю за отраву;
Но этот Муравей был не такого нраву:
Он их любил,
Своим их чванством мерил
И всем им верил:
А ими наконец так голову набил,
Что вздумал в город показаться,
Чтоб силой там повеличаться.
На самый крупный с сеном воз
Он к мужику спесиво всполз
И въехал в город очень пышно;
Но, ах, какой для гордости удар!
Он думал, на него сбежится весь базар,
Как на пожар;
А про него совсем не слышно:
У всякого забота там своя.
Мой Муравей, то взяв листок, потянет,
То припадет он, то привстанет :
Никто не видит Муравья.
Уставши наконец тянуться, выправляться,
С досадою Барбосу он сказал,
Который у воза хозяйского лежал:
"Не правда ль, надобно признаться,
Что в городе у вас
Народ без толку и без глаз?
Возможно ль, что меня никто не примечает,
Как ни тянусь я целый час;
А кажется, у нас
Меня весь муравейник знает".
И со стыдом отправился домой.

Так думает иной
Затейник,
Что он в подсолнечной гремит,
А он – дивит
Свой только муравейник.

The Ant

Within his hill a certain Ant was famed for strength.
He lifted barley grains three times his length.
His courage far surpassed the hero ants of yore
(Or so the ant historians all swore).
And any foe of ants he'd fearlessly attack:
Let worms and spiders come – he stopped them in their track.
And, if they didn't stop, he tore them limb from limb.
Of course, such deeds were much admired.
Within the hill the talk was all of him.
Though I, myself, of praise would soon grow tired,
He reveled in the homage he'd inspired.
He, naturally, believed it all was true
And every word was just his due.
Deciding that his gifts demanded wider view,
In his conceit, he thought he'd leave the hill
And go to town to give its folks a thrill.
He hitched there in a wagon full of hay
And dreamed of further triumphs all the way.
But when he got there, what a blow to find
That no one paid him any mind.
(He'd thought that he was known throughout the land,
And that the town would come to meet him with a band.)
Instead he found himself unknown,
And folks concerned with business of their own.
He tried to get attention anyway
By putting his great power on display.
And so he grabbed a leaf – the heaviest he'd found –
And raised it high, then pumped it up and down.
Yet no crowds of townsmen came around
To watch his feat of strength with awe.
Indeed, you'd think that no one even saw.
At last he stopped, exhausted,
Discouraged and disgusted,
And went back home in bitterness and shame.
For this he held the townsfolk all to blame
For being blind to what at home brought him such fame.

Thus, someone who by kin is glorified,
May think that he is famous far and wide.
And yet his much-praised strength or art or skill
Impresses only ants in his small hill.

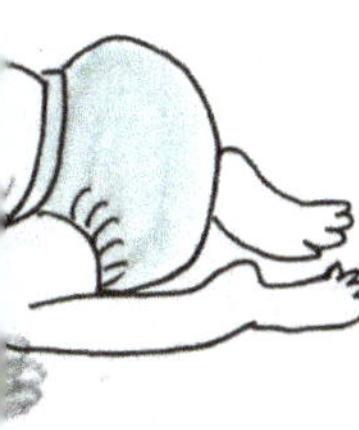

Осёл и Соловей

Осёл увидел Соловья
И говорит ему: “Послушай – ка, дружище!
Ты, сказывают, петь великий мастерище.
Хотел бы очень я
Сам посудить, твоё услышав пенье,
Велико ль подлинно твоё уменье?”
Тут Соловей являть своё искусство стал:
Защёлкал, засвистал
На тысячу ладов, тянул, переливался;
То нежно он ослабевал
И томной вдалеке свирелью отдавался,
То мелкой дробью вдруг по роще рассыпался.
Внимало всё тогда
Любимцу и певцу Авроры:
Затихли ветерки, замолкли птичек хоры,
И прилегли стада
Чуть – чуть дыша, пастух им любовался
И только иногда,
Внимая Соловью, пастушке улыбался.
Скончал певец. Осёл, уставясь в землю лбом:
“Изрядно, – говорит, – сказать неложно,
Тебя без скуки слушать можно;
А жаль, что незнаком
Ты с нашим петухом;
Ещё б ты боле навострился,
Когда бы у него немножко поучился”.
Услыша суд такой, мой бедный Соловей
Вспорхнул – и полетел за тридевять полей.
Избави, Бог, и нас от этаких судей.

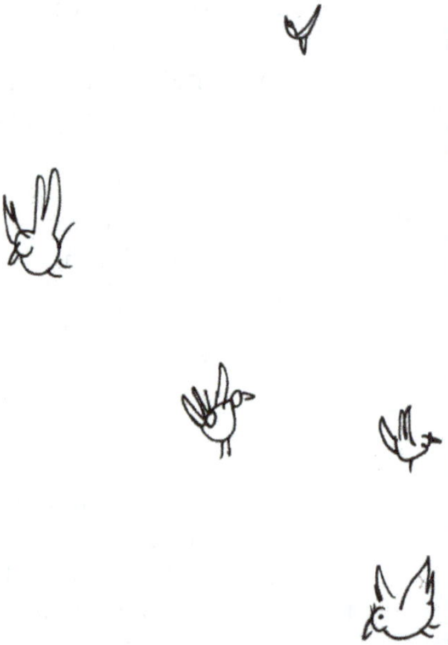

The Ass and the Nightingale

An Ass once met a Nightingale
And said, "My friend, I've heard a tale.
They say you sing like no one else.
I'd dearly love to hear you for myself.
I'm quite a judge of singing, don't you know,
And want to see if what they say is so."
So Nightingale began to show his art.
He gave a lovely warble for a start,
A really stunning tremolo.
Then his voice began to soar,
Then dipped, then reached the heights once more,
And next a lullaby he crooned,
As all the forest nearly swooned.
And from his very first sweet trill,
All life within the wood stood still,
As all its creatures strove to hear
The wondrous sounds resounding here.
The breezes stopped their blowing;
The cattle stopped their lowing;
The shepherdess was full of sighs;
And tears came to the shepherd's eyes.
And at the concert's termination
They all were dumb with admiration;
Except the Ass, who showed his wit
And said, "Not bad, I wasn't bored a bit!
But all the same,
It is a shame,
You've never come to visit at our farm.
Some pointers from our cock would do no harm.
Indeed, I think they'd be just what you need,
To really bring your singing up to speed."
The Nightingale took off above the trees.
God save us all from critics such as these.

Осёл и Мужик

Мужик на лето в огород
Наняв Осла, приставил
Ворон и воробьёв гонять нахальный род.
Осёл был самых честных правил:
Ни с хищностью, ни с кражей незнаком,
Не поживился он хозяйским ни листком
И птицам, грех сказать, чтобы давал потачку;
Но Мужику барыш был с огорода плох.
Осёл, гоняя птиц, со всех ослиных ног,
По всем грядам и вдоль и поперёк
Такую поднял скачку,
Что в огороде всё примял и притоптал.
Увидя тут, что труд его пропал,
Крестьянин на спине ослиной
Убыток выместил дубиной.
"И ништо! – все кричат, – скотине поделом!
С его ль умом
За это дело браться?"

А я скажу, не с тем, чтоб за Осла вступаться;
Он, точно, виноват (с ним сделан и расчёт),
Но, кажется, не прав и тот,
Кто поручил Ослу стеречь свой огород

The Ass and the Peasant

A peasant with a veggie plot,
From fear that birds would take a lot,
Decided 'twould be wise to pay
A guard to keep the birds away.
But help was hard to find. Alas,
No one applied except an Ass.
So he was hired for this work.
To tell the truth, he didn't shirk.
An honest Ass, his zeal was ample,
But none had taught him not to trample.
The garden was churned up – a mess.
The profit from it came to less
Than if the birds had had their share.
The Peasant, mad, began to swear
And beat the ass with all his might.
His neighbors said, "It serves Ass right,
He should have known he isn't smart enough
To undertake a job this tough."

Though I'd not argue in the beast's defense,
He is at fault (his back paid recompense).
I think the Peasant also bears his share of blame.
'Twas he who did the hiring, all the same.

Заяц на ловле

Большой собравшися гурьбой,
Медведя звери изловили;
На чистом поле задавили –
И делят меж собой,
Кто что себе достанет.
А Заяц за ушко медвежье тут же тянет.
"Ба, ты, косой, –
Кричат ему, – пожаловал отколе?
Тебя никто на ловле не видал". –
"Вот, братцы! – Заяц отвечал, –
Да из лесу – то кто ж, – всё я его пугал
И к вам поставил прямо в поле
Сердечного дружка?"
Такое хвастовство хоть слишком было явно,
Но показалось так забавно,
Что Зайцу дан клочок медвежьего ушка
.
Над хвастунами хоть смеются,
А часто в дележе им доли достаются.

The Hare and the Hunt

Some animals, poor hunters all,
Began to wonder whether
Their luck would change, more game would fall,
Were they to hunt together.
On their first hunt they killed a bear,
Much to their own surprise.
Each hunter was to get a share –
Bear meat for stews and pies.
When suddenly up came a Hare
And tried to stake a claim.
The others cried, "You weren't there;
You didn't hunt! For shame!"
"But, brothers," boldly Hare replied.
"I did; I was the one
Who crept into Bear's lair,
And gave him such a scare
That right toward you he chanced to run."
The others laughed until they cried,
But gave Bear's ear to Bunny.
Because, though, clearly, he had lied,
They found his boasts so funny.

The whole world mocks a boastful Hare,
Yet frequently he gets his share.

Волк и Пастухи

Волк, близко обходя пастуший двор
И видя, сквозь забор,
Что, выбрав лучшего себе барана в стаде,
Спокойно Пастухи барашка потрошат,
А псы смирнёхонько лежат,
Сам молвил про себя, прочь уходя в досаде:
“Какой бы шум вы все здесь подняли, друзья,
Когда бы это сделал я!”

The Wolf and the Shepherds

Attracted by a smell delicious and intense –
The smell of mutton being charred –
A Wolf approached a Shepherds' yard
And peeked in through the fence.
A sight to make him weep:
On a spit the flock's most luscious sheep,
While sheepdogs lay there calmly half asleep.
Said Wolf, "Oh, what a noise you'd all have raised,
If I had caught that sheep and had him braised."

Winged Phrases • Крылатые Фразы

Quotes from fables in this collection that have become aphorisms in Russian

The Ant
А он — дивит
Свой только муравейник.
And yet his much-praised strength or art or skill
Impresses only ants in his small hill.

The Ass and the Nightingale
А жаль, что незнаком
Ты с нашим петухом.
It is a shame,
You never came to visit at our farm.
Some pointers from our cock would do no harm.

Избави бог и нас от этаких судей.
God save us all from critics such as these.

The Cat and the Cook
А Васька слушает да ест.
Now Vaska meekly listened, as befits a sinner;
Repentantly he sighed, but kept on eating dinner.

The Cat and the Nightingale
Худые песни Соловью
В когтях у Кошки
You can't expect to hear sweet songs
From birds trapped where no bird belongs —
Within the clutches of a Cat.

The Crow
Ворона в павлиных перьях
A crow in peacock feathers.

Ни Пава, ни Ворона
For though she was no Peacock, nor was she a Crow.

The Cuckoo and the Rooster
Кукушка хвалит Петуха?
За то, что хвалит он Кукушку
Thus, Rooster praises Cuckoo so she'll do the same.

The Dragonfly and the Ants
Стрекоза уж не поёт;
И кому же в ум пойдёт
На желудок петь голодный!
Then Dragonfly felt hunger's pang.
And, no surprise, no longer sang.

Как под каждым ей листком
Был готов и стол и дом.
(When) Beneath each leaf more food she found.
And shelter too.

Ты всё пела? Это дело:
Так поди же, попляши!"
Well then, perhaps what you should do,"
Replied the Ants,
"Is dance."

The Eagle and the Bee
Что в них и моего хоть капля мёду есть.
I know that mine are there, and do not wish for more.

The Eagle and the Chickens
Орлам случается и ниже Кур спускаться;
Но Курам никогда до облак не подняться!
At times we Eagles may at Chicken level fly.
But more important: it is true
That Chickens never ever reach the heights we do.

The Eagle and the Mole
Не презирай совета ничьего,
Но прежде рассмотри его.
Examine well-meant counsel case by case—
Do not disdain it, even though its source is base.

The Elephant and the Pug
Ай, Моська! знать, она сильна,
Что лает на Слона
Here's Pug, who's brave and confident
And challenged a huge Elephant.

The Flowers
Одни поддельные цветы
Дождя боятся.
And only artificial flowers feel
Afraid of rain

The Crow and the Fox
От радости в зобу дыханье спёрло.
Her mind was in a whirl, her breath caught in her crop.

Уж сколько раз твердили миру,
Что лесть гнусна, вредна.
It's often said and each of us agrees
That flattery does harm and is a scoundrel's art.

The Vixen and the Woodchuck
Рыльце в пуху.
Feathers on your chin.

The Geese
Да наши предки Рим спасли!
Our forebears rescued Rome!

Да чтоб гусей не раздразнить.
But geese when riled are such a pain.

The Greedy Man and the Hen
Скупой теряет всё, желая всё достать.
Although they have enough, the greedy strive for more
And often thereby lose what wealth they have in store.

The Lion on a Hunt
Львиная доля
The Lion's share

The Monkey and the Looking Glass
Чем кумушек считать трудиться,
Не лучше ль на себя, кума, оборотиться?
Now, counting flaws in friends won't get you anywhere!
Best think about what makes your own self less than fair!

The Monkey and the Spectacles
Мартышка к старости слаба глазами стала.
Miss Monkey's eyes began to fail as she got old.

The Mouse and the Rat
Не радуйся, мой свет,
И не надейся по-пустому!
I fear rejoicing's premature.
The Lion won't survive, of that I'm sure.

Сильнее кошки зверя нет.
No creature in the world could overcome Cat's paw.

The Musicians
Они немножечко дерут:
Зато уж в рот хмельного не берут.
Well, yes, I know their singing stinks,
And, yet, not one among them drinks.

А я скажу: по мне уж лучше пей,
Да дело разумей.
Myself, I'd rather men who might get tight,
But had the proper skills to do things right.

The Passersby and the Dogs
Полают, да отстанут.
They'll yelp a bit and then shut up.

The Rooster and the Pearl
Жемчужное зерно в навозной куче
A pearl in a dung heap

Навозну кучу разрывая,
Петух нашёл Жемчужное зерно
While pecking in a compost mound,
A rooster came upon a pearl.

The Sow Beneath the Oak
Свинья под дубом.
Sow beneath the oak.

The Squirrel
Как Белка в колесе.
Like that Squirrel in the wheel.

String Quartet
Мы, верно, уж поладим,
Коль рядом сядем
If we sit thus, our music cannot flow.
The secret is we must sit in a row.

А вы, друзья, как ни садитесь,
Всё в музыканты не годитесь.
To make fine music there's no way that you'll be fit,
My friends, no matter how you sit.'

The Swan, the Pike and the Crab
Когда в товарищах согласья нет,
На лад их дело не пойдёт.
When members of a team cannot agree;
Though each one labors conscientiously,
They'll not complete the task they've started on.

Да Лебедь рвётся в облака,
Рак пятится назад, а Щука тянет в воду.
The Pike sought water, Swan of course the sky;
While Crab a sideways course did ply.

Да только воз и ныне там.
As for the cart – it never budged.

The Titmouse
Наделала Синица славы,
А моря не зажгла.
Though she had gained some fame (unearned).
As for the sea—it never burned.

The Treasure Chest
А Ларчик просто открывался.
You simply raise its lid, like any other chest.

The Two Barrel Carts
Кто про свои дела кричит всем без умолку,
В том, верно, мало толку.
A person who talks and talks about his every deed
Is liable to be one we need not heed.

The Two Dogs
Как счастье многие находят
Лишь тем, что хорошо на задних лапках ходят!
Men, too, win favor, fame, applause
If they can walk on their hind paws.

The Wolf and the Shepherds
Какой бы шум вы все здесь подняли, друзья,
Когда бы это сделал я!
Oh, what a noise you'd all have raised.
If I had caught that sheep and had it braised.

The Wolf and His Cub
Да сам пастух дурак;
А где пастух дурак, там и собаки дуры.
The shepherd is a fool. And when that's true,
It follows that the dogs must be fools too."